Praise for *Internal Jiu Jitsu*

"A martial arts book for the modern era, *Internal Jiu Jitsu* is a bridge between the dojo and the real world that artfully weaves the practice of jiu jitsu with the journey of life. Julio Rivera breaks down the barriers between the physical and mental game so that it's hard to tell where fight training ends and mental wellness begins."

– **DAVE STERN** author of *Hackproof Your Startup*, entrepreneur

"*Internal Jiu Jitsu* is a handy field guide for facing and managing the many external and self-imposed challenges we face in life, both on and off the mat."

– **NICK MEYER** student of Julio's, owner of Eckhart Beer Co., Brooklyn

"Julio Rivera, NYC martial arts and fitness legend, connects the dots between martial arts and life in *Internal Jiu Jitsu* — thought provoking, transformative, and eternal."

– **ALEX ECKLIN** 3rd degree BJJ black belt, Masterskya founder

"*Internal Jiu Jitsu* is not only an honest depiction of what it's like to live with bipolar disorder, but a story of ongoing resilience relevant to all. As a mental health professional, I recommend *Internal Jiu Jitsu* to anyone seeking to develop deeper self-awareness in caring for one's mental well being."

– **MARIA PAGAN** PhD, LCSW, therapist and mental health advocate

"I could not put this book down. Julio's stories are riveting, and the key takeaways help the reader retain the points made in each chapter. *Internal Jiu Jitsu* will help guide you as a martial artist and guide you through the steps you need to conquer yourself."

– **BENJAMIN J. COLEMAN** Music educator, clarinetist, judo black belt

"I highly recommend anyone who trains, has trained, or is an instructor, to please pick up a copy and read *Internal Jiu Jitsu* from beginning to end."

— **DESPINA KALLERGIS** Jiu jitsu practitioner

"10/10 recommend — whether you're into martial arts or just tired of trying to strong-arm your way through everything."

— **LEE YUZARY** Licensed clinical social worker, recognized in *Marquis Who's Who* (2022)

INTERNAL JIU JITSU

Conquering Mind and Body Resistance by Giving Way

Julio Angel Rivera

Published by How2Conquer
Atlanta, Georgia
www.how2conquer.com

How2Conquer is an imprint of White Deer Publishing, LLC.
www.whitedeerpublishing.net

© 2025 by Julio Angel Rivera

All rights reserved. No part of this publication may be reproduced, stored in a retrieval system, or transmitted in any form or by any means — for example, electronic, photocopy, recording — without the prior written permission of the publisher. The only exception is brief quotations in printed reviews.

First edition, May 2025
Ebook edition created 2025

Illustrations and cover design by Telia Garner
Edited by Lauren Kelliher, Charlotte Bleau

Library of Congress Cataloging-in-Publication Data is on file at the Library of Congress, Washington, DC.

Print ISBN 978-1-945783-43-2
Ebook ISBN 978-1-945783-44-9

For information about special discounts available for bulk purchases, please contact How2Conquer Special Sales at www.how2conquer.com/bulk-orders.

Use of this book for the purposes of training generative artificial intelligence (AI) technologies is prohibited. The author reserves exclusive rights to license or give specific and express permission to do so.

For Mama

Contents

Preface: What is Jiu Jitsu? v

Foreword 1

Introduction 3

Section 1: Letting Go of Resistance 7

Chapter 1: The Back Office 9

Chapter 2: Being in the Moment 15

Chapter 3: Confronting Your Fear 19

Chapter 4: (Not) Reacting 23

Chapter 5: The Standing Dance 27

Chapter 6: Transitions 31

Section 2: Training Your Trauma 35

Chapter 7: Jiu Jitsu Your Life 37

Chapter 8: Trauma and the Kung Fu Master 43

Chapter 9: Self-Defense vs. Self-Empowerment 47

Chapter 10: Confidence and Combat Sports 51

Section 3: Finding the Right Angle 57

Chapter 11: Judging Books by Their Covers 59

Chapter 12: Rolling through Danger 63

Chapter 13: Knowing When to Tap 67

Chapter 14: Competition and Fear 71

Chapter 15: Butterflies Are Your Friends 77

Chapter 16: Wanting to Quit 81

i

Section 4: Committing to Yourself 87

Chapter 17: Hammers and Nails 89

Chapter 18: Playing Hurt 95

Chapter 19: Getting over the Hump 101

Chapter 20: The Black Belt 105

Chapter 21: The Arm Collectors 109

Section 5: Choosing Your Community 113

Chapter 22: Choosing the Right Academy 115

Chapter 23: Picking the Right Partners 119

Chapter 24: Loyalty 125

Wrap Up & Resources 131

Conclusion: Post Training 133

Resources 137

Acknowledgments 139

About the Author 141

What is Jiu Jitsu?

The Evolution

Jiu jitsu, or the gentle art, was the hand-to-hand fighting system of the samurai in feudal Japan.[1] The art was designed to fight when weapons weren't available and relied on throws, joint locks, and strangulations to defeat an opponent on the battlefield.

With the fall of the samurai in Japan, society frowned upon the associated jiu jitsu, so its practice dwindled. Still, dojos existed, some with attached bone-setting clinics for when practitioners were injured in training.

Professor Jigoro Kano, an educator and jiu jitsu practitioner, set out to develop his own style (Kano jiu jitsu), which could be practiced at full intensity without causing bodily harm. Kano's system came to be known as judo (the gentle way in Japanese), and it eliminated many of the more dangerous or impractical techniques of the original jiu jitsu styles, allowing it to be practiced safely.[2]

Kano's students dominated in challenge matches against other jiu jitsu schools, and his style became the martial art of Japan's police force in 1866. As a respected private school professor and a champion of physical fitness in Japan, Kano's influence and notoriety propelled judo to prominence. Judo became a part of the Japanese education system in 1911, as Kano's vision was that the sport and its principles would benefit all of humanity. In 2012, martial arts, including judo, became mandatory in Japanese schools.

In the early twentieth century, one of Kano's students, Mitsuyo Maeda, traveled the world having no-rules challenge matches against fighters of any style. Eventually, Maeda settled in Brazil, and got help establishing himself there from a politician named Gastão Gracie. As repayment, Maeda taught Gracie's son judo, which was still generally called jiu jitsu.

The Gracie family named their style Gracie jiu jitsu, which gave birth to the more modern Brazilian jiu jitsu that's practiced today. These styles focus more on ground fighting than traditional jiu jitsu or judo and became more popular after the explosive growth of the Ultimate Fighting Championship (UFC).

As a black belt in traditional jiu jitsu, judo, and Brazilian jiu jitsu, I simply refer to all of them as jiu jitsu for the purposes of this book. The principles are the same, although the favored techniques and applications vary.

Key Takeaways

1 Jiu jitsu was the fighting style of the samurai in feudal Japan, relying on leverage, throws, joint locks, and strangulations to defeat an opponent without weapons.

2 Jigoro Kano turned his style into what he called judo, a safer way to practice jiu jitsu at full intensity.

3 Judo evolved into Brazilian jiu jitsu after Mitsuyo Maeda taught Carlos Gracie.

Foreword

GINNY: Your body's kind of banged up, isn't it?
MAYNARD: You should see the inside.

— *2 Very Dangerous People Sharing 1 Small Space, A Play*[3]

    My father signed me up for karate training when I was eleven or twelve. He got into it at the same time, even though he was middle-aged by then. He idolized Chuck Norris, so it had been his dream to study karate, and he leaped into it. He faced more challenges than most.

    See, my father had been crippled by polio when he was four years old, and his left leg did not work the same as most legs. It was incredibly weak. That did not deter him, though he had to work twice as hard as we did, and after two years, his leg got stronger. It would never be the same as his right leg; it would always be damaged, but it was also stronger, and so was my father, due to his study of karate.

    We all carry scars from growing up; I have one on my thigh, the result of a climbing accident gone wrong, and another on my lip due to an unfortunate connection with the wrong end of a baseball bat when I was thirteen. That scar is barely visible nowadays, decades later, but it's there if one looks for it.

    Those are just the visible scars, mind you. There are others on the inside.

    I've been studying various martial arts for the majority of my life. During that time I've come to know many martial artists in a vast array of disciplines from locations around the world. One commonality between them? Something happened that made them wish to train: an incident, a conflict, a fight, or any manner of an unfortunate experience. Something awful and traumatic. There's a reason my father signed me up for karate: I was getting beat up every day at school, and when I say beat up, I mean beaten for real. Back then, boys and young men were expected, if not encouraged, to fight each other for sport in public school.

While the damage on the outside was minimal, the damage to the spirit, the emotional center of who I was, was devastating. It scarred me far worse than that collision with the baseball bat. It hurt my humanity. And, as bad as I had it, over the years, I saw others endure far worse, not just from fellow students, but from adults, bad actors, and predators.

The fascinating thing about the study and training of martial arts is that they don't just heal and strengthen my body . . . they also do the same for my spirit. Karate, judo, taekwondo, boxing, and jiu jitsu began to heal my core emotional being. It's a journey of healing that continues to this day. It's the reason I continue to train.

Martial arts isn't only about the body. It's about the connection between the mind, the body, and the spirit. Sensei Julio, whom I've known and trained with for fifteen years, understands this intrinsically. He can speak on this topic with more knowledge and breadth than I can and is one of the few martial artists I've known who readily admits to the scars carried on the soul. You can't fix one without the other, and you can't defend one while ignoring the other and be successful as a martial artist. You cannot.

Sensei Julio provides a helpful guide for those of us who train while also navigating injuries to the soul.

Don't just train your body, train your spirit and soul, too.

—**JOSHUA TODD JAMES** *is an author and martial artist. He's written the novels* SOME ANIMALS, MINORITY OF ONE, FREEDOM RUN, MAN IN A BOX, RENEGADE, *and more, as well as the action films* Pound of Flesh *and* Take Cover. *He holds black belts in taekwondo, American kickboxing, and Brazilian jiu jitsu.*

Introduction

Internal jiu jitsu isn't physical, but it requires the ability to think in tangible terms. Envisioning the back-and-forth pressure applied during a struggle — and recognizing when to push or pull — doesn't happen by chance. It takes practice to get good at noticing the subtle changes in yourself and your adversary (or obstacle) that could cause massive movement in one direction or the other.

Mindfulness and awareness are the only ways to master internal jiu jitsu. To sense what's happening around and inside you, you must listen, watch, and feel in the present. Being stuck in the past or projecting into the future pulls you away from connecting with life. Just like losing your grip during a match, without that connection, you've lost both control and guidance. You have no partner to base your own movement on. There is nothing for you to respond to. You're on your own.

When I first opened my own academy in 2009, my focus was on the physical side of martial arts, while still placing emphasis on the discipline instilled by training. It took me another decade to begin to see how jiu jitsu was connected to everything else in my life.

While working with my students in a capacity far more expansive than that of an instructor, I was privy to their dreams and concerns, as well as to how their training could be applied to their issues. The closeness I had with my students afforded me the opportunity to help them on and off the mat. Since selling my school in 2018, writing has allowed me to extend my teaching beyond the academy doors.

Over time I came to see that by understanding balance, leverage, and force, you can use what first appears as a roadblock to propel you in another direction. Fighting force with force — denying the power that you are up against — takes away your ability to use that energy to your advantage. The resistance life seems to offer can power your journey, if you accept it.

A black belt can take a decade or more to earn, but the lessons of the rank are learned over a lifetime. To paraphrase the great Ralph Macchio as the original "Karate Kid," we learn to fight so we don't have to fight. We learn to use opposing energy rather than resist it — to fight without fighting.

We can't make the battle going on inside of us into a bloody war. Only we will suffer. We have to fight strategically, based on all the information we have about our opposition, in this case, ourselves.

There's a lifetime of intel inside all of us to help us conquer our inner enemy. The first step might be not seeing them as the enemy at all.

SECTION 1: LETTING GO OF RESISTANCE

"Today is victory over yourself of yesterday; tomorrow is your victory over lesser men."

— Miyamoto Musashi, *The Book of Five Rings*

CHAPTER 1
The Back Office

In 2019, I tried to hang myself in a basement with the monogrammed black belt it took me years to earn. Twenty years earlier, I'd started building the skills that got me through life after the belt gave way.

At the back of a narrow, wood-paneled storefront, with worn out bags hanging from steel chains and the damp smell of hard work in the air, there was a serenely decorated office where my sensei was only concerned with one's inner world. This was a place to practice Internal Jiu Jitsu.

Six months into my training, my sensei literally began acting as my therapist, with weekly sessions in that serene back office. Martial arts and mental health have been intertwined for me ever since. I used my training on the mat to let out my physical energy, and the therapy to explore my inner world.

Before that, I was focused exclusively on the outer. Competitive bodybuilding was my release. Instead of exploring my feelings, the weights got the brunt of my anger and gave me physical pain that reflected my inner anguish. But combat sports offered much more. It wasn't just me against the weights in the pursuit of cosmetic perfection. I had to both conquer my own fear and overcome my opponent. When I began sparring in jiu jitsu and boxing, I learned my determination had to come from a deeper place than it did in the weight room because of the heightened intensity of a fight — even a friendly one.

The inevitable bumps, bruises, fractures, and concussions in combat sports might be considered masochistic, but practitioners just see those things as unfortunate occurrences that are part of the game.

I'm sure there's a deeper meaning. Maybe part of us needs to feel some pain all the time.

My father always urged me to give up my physical endeavors whenever I got injured. The scarcity and chronic pain he grew up with instilled a fear in him that I didn't understand until I got older. He was risk-averse, while I was drawn to adventure.

Dad's warnings were sometimes justified. Like when I was thirteen years old, and he advised me not to go to a party around the corner from our building because it was dangerous. I argued that it was only a block and a half away, and I'd be back by 10pm. Sure enough, I was robbed at gunpoint that night. Dad was right, but if I'd listened to every warning, I would've been the boy in the bubble. I felt my dad's fear, but I also felt compelled to work through it because it was such an emotional burden. I knew that being afraid could stop me from living the life I wanted. My main mission on Earth was to conquer my fear.

Fighting seemed like a good place to start. As my twenty-fourth birthday approached, I was finally ready to confront my fear head on. I was terrified of violence because I'd been around it so much. I'd fought a lot as a kid out of necessity because it was what was expected in my neighborhood. You either fought or you were a punk. I hated it. I wanted to become friends with the feeling of terror before a fight. If I couldn't avoid the sensation, then I wanted to try to enjoy it.

That fear doesn't just happen prior to throwing hands or locking up in a wrestling match. The terror of what's to come can strike before a speech, a first date, or a job interview. Learning to manage the symptoms associated with stress and anxiety should be a major goal of any practice.

Why Fighting Applies to All of Us

As different as we all are, we're also remarkably similar. Our emotional states aren't uniquely our own. Sadness, joy, despair, happiness, hopelessness — we all experience them. Where we are on

Chapter 1: The Back Office

the spectrum of those emotions varies, but we all know exactly how they feel — at least to each of us.

Controlling one's emotions is an integral part of most disciplines. Whether slowing your heart rate in archery, focusing on a 90-mph fastball headed straight for your face in baseball, or controlling your anger in a fight, emotional regulation plays a significant role in high-stress activities.

Martial arts, when applied practically, create a greater understanding of resistance and the difference between reacting and responding — answering in the present rather than in the past or future.

This type of resistance isn't just physical. To paraphrase Steven Pressfield's brilliant book, *The War of Art*, we all face resistance every day. It's a constant battle to overcome the internal forces that insist on taking us down.

Of the many ways to do this, martial arts suited me best. For you, it may be something completely different, but the spirit will be the same. You will work through plateaus and exhaustion using will and determination, but not just through brute force. Artistry requires more than that.

An obstacle that can't be averted must be coerced, manipulated — seduced into relaxing its defenses. In pulling at the things I want; I cause them to move away defensively. If I pushed assertively, then they would lean toward me in an effort to stand their ground.

Push someone away and their own defensiveness can draw them to you. Reject someone's offer and they might react by coming on stronger. Whether in business or romance, people are often attracted to what they can't have. Their stubbornness may motivate them to prove you wrong.

It takes some finesse to set up an opponent to move the way you want them to. Using strength alone can't always win an altercation, and cunning makes the challenge less demanding. In manipulating someone physically, pushing buttons and pulling levers is how you test what their reactions will be. Like the feints and fakes of boxing, your goal is to get them to bite like a fish, before you pull them the opposite way — into your grasp.

If I want to throw you forward in judo, I'll start by explosively pushing you back so you adjust your own body forward. I want you to do most of the work. I'm not looking to use my strength to pull your weight. That would require exponentially more energy.

When I'm fighting with myself, either with negative thoughts or self-destructive behavior, I know that sustained aggression isn't the answer. I need to give way to the emotions — to acknowledge and accept them. Berating myself into doing better only takes me back to early feelings of inadequacy and failure. I'm pushing too hard to get the reaction I want. All I really need is one sharp jolt to get me going in the right direction.

Like so many of us, I never felt like I was doing or being enough. A B grade at school was cause for disappointment. Only winning one trophy at a bodybuilding competition was underachieving. I once hesitated to go home and considered buying myself a trophy when my breakdancing routine didn't win the school talent show.

I'd give myself an emotional and mental beating whenever I felt like a failure. Having ADHD meant motivation and focus for things I wasn't passionate about was hard to come by. There were a dozen TVs at full volume in my head.

A debate that devolves into a screaming match, whether in the inner or outer world, is a prize fight that has broken down into a brawl. Random fists flying all over the place, with little direction or technique, makes for an ugly display that proves no real point. Nothing is resolved, except maybe who is the loudest or what thought can drown out the others while still being unintelligible. There is no style in this type of solution — no artistry.

Artistic fighting isn't chaos, as chaotic as it may seem. Great fighting is carefully crafted — expertly set up before being precisely executed. It's a game of chess with higher stakes.

Our internal fight should also be artistically approached. Things shouldn't be forced. We should feel where we are resisting most and push back just enough to judge our reactions. We need to set ourselves up to make progress and take action to create momentum, even if it means taking a step back first.

The last thing anyone needs is a brawl in their head. If I hadn't walked into that back office 20 years ago, then I might have never really learned how to fight my inner battle. And while jiu jitsu has trained my body well, its effect of on my mental health has been even greater.

Key Takeaways

1 Inner and outer resistance can be approached in the same way.

2 By giving just the right amount of pushback, we may get the reaction we are looking for.

3 Forward motion starts action, and movement leads to progress.

CHAPTER 2
Being in the Moment

The gentle art isn't what you'd expect the practice of breaking bones and rendering someone unconscious to be called, yet the name perfectly describes the theory behind jiu jitsu. Like the principle of wu wei in Taoism, where one goes with the flow of nature, jiu jitsu is the practice of going with the resistance you are facing. It's the opposite of pointlessly struggling against what is.

To practice jiu jitsu, you must be in the moment. Your responses are based on the connection you have with your opponent. The most subtle movements create opportunities for victory. If you aren't fully aware of what's happening, you may anticipate incorrectly, and fall into a trap. Basing your strategy solely on the past instead of in the moment will leave you anticipating something that never comes. Staying present makes you sensitive to the slightest fluctuations, so you can be guided by real-time feedback.

Being lost in one's own thoughts is counter to jiu jitsu. Isolating yourself from your surroundings will cut you off from your source of information. Trapped in your own head, you won't know what your opponent is doing — and you won't be able to respond.

Depression and anxiety can lead to the same type of suffocating isolation. Unsure of what's happening in the outside world, we have no idea what moving parts could be helping us out of our funk. We're disconnected from the world we see as our opponent.

But it's that very opponent's actions and reactions that will dictate the direction you should take. The path of least resistance is revealed by the very opposition you think holds you back. Obstacles block one path and push you toward another.

"Fire may fight with water,
But heat and moisture generate all things,
Their discord being productive."

— Ovid, *Metamorphoses*[4]

Life and martial arts are both dances where partners alternate leading and following. Neither one has a distinct advantage over the other — both equally capable of winning from either position. The rhythm of fighting encompasses the action. In the constant kinetic exchange of energy, sparks fly, like a "bang" or "boom" sound-effect balloons in the old *Batman* TV series. In jiu jitsu, those sparks can be created from an infinite number of positions, and the person that finishes on their back can be the decisive victor.

Discomfort and Surrender

The positions we're pushed into by life are often uncomfortable, but discomfort doesn't mean defeat. In the most contorted position, a jiu jitsu practitioner can find just the right angle to gain an advantage. With enough skill and technique, what looks to be doom can quickly turn into a spectacular win. Knowledge and the right attitude will bring a solution, even if that solution is ultimately tapping out. (Read more in **Chapter 13: Knowing When to Tap**.)

That's another lesson from jiu jitsu. There must be times when you're willing to admit you're beaten. You must occasionally surrender. There's no shame in admitting defeat when you've fought valiantly. Humility is something you learn on your first day at a jiu jitsu academy.

In jiu jitsu it's said that some days you're the nail and some days you're the hammer. When our minds have worn us down, it's often tough to admit we're playing the nail that day. Unlike in jiu jitsu, life allows you to pretend. You can do something flashy to detract from the substance, and never have your assertions tested. You can hide.

A facade can shield a couple of layers of a person's true self, allowing them to get by undetected on anyone's bullshit meter. Facades don't hold up on the mat.

Hiding is just being defensive. It's curling up into the turtle position (kneeling on all fours) and holding on for dear life, hoping your opponent doesn't tie you into knots until the bell rings.

Still, sometimes all you can do is turtle — hide in your shell. You don't have another answer.

Other times you try to force a technique that isn't there. Your opponent is insisting on going one way, and you are insisting on going another. Now, you're not doing jiu jitsu. You're trying too hard. You aren't going with what you're being given. You're resisting what is.

When we insist on always fighting the way things are, with no real plan on how to go another direction, we waste energy. Jigoro Kano, the founder of judo, said his art was meant for mutual benefit and maximum efficiency. Through utilizing all the power of our opponent's resistance, we are propelled into new possibilities. Fear of this power keeps us stiff, defensive, and unwilling to attack.

Being frozen by fear is something most of us face at some point, particularly when there's a major decision to be made. Non-action in the wu wei sense doesn't mean doing nothing. If the wind pushes you, you allow it to guide you. You don't insist on swimming upstream if you wish to travel efficiently, and you don't anchor yourself to the ground and refuse to move.

Fighting against feelings is the same. Rather than reacting irrationally and falling into a trap, determine if you're being pushed or pulled by your emotions. Maximize your efficiency. Go where your feelings take you, but do it consciously. Know you can win if you find the right angle. From that point, a fresh perspective emerges, and how you perceive each moment is as important as the moment itself.

Key Takeaways

1 Jiu jitsu is played the way life should be. Be in the moment and go with the flow.

2 Obstacles can help guide you.

3 Resistance has the power to propel you to new possibilities.

4 A new angle will give you a different perspective.

CHAPTER 3
Confronting Your Fear

For many of us, life feels less safe than we remember from our youth. For some of us, it never felt safe.

Every day, it seems unending press coverage of another tragic event is creating a culture dominated by fear. The anxiety of actual danger has piled on to the unrelenting pressure that we already put on ourselves as human beings.

When you grow up around violence, like I did, it becomes normalized, but not normal. You feel like that's just the way things are everywhere because it's all you've seen, but it never feels right.

Before I was out of grade school, two people I knew were killed for being good Samaritans. One of them was a stranger I only knew by the look in his eyes as he lay dying in the street.

The victim in the other incident was a family friend who the neighborhood was proud of for joining the Marine Corps. I can still see the wallet sized photo my mom had of him in his military dress. He was stabbed to death for defending a girl in the park. These were dangerous parks.

Living in that neighborhood had me on edge all the time. I was programmed that way.

Even when things seem peaceful, the body of a trauma survivor remembers fear and is always on alert. I once thought I'd always be afraid. So, although I became a champion bodybuilder and martial artist, I still lived in fear — until I confronted it. It wasn't an overnight process.

We can all feel safer by acknowledging our fear and using its energy to empower ourselves. It comes down to perspective.

The chemicals our bodies produce in response to danger are the same whether that danger is real or imagined. Interpreting the sensations associated with fear and anxiety as negative blocks us from efficiently using the boost in alertness and physical strength our bodies naturally provide for protection in times of stress.

A shift in mindset can change how you feel walking down the street. Realizing what's happening inside your body during times of stress can demystify fear and anxiety and provide relief.

A better understanding of the anatomy of violence, the role of trauma and defensiveness in conflict, and the power of empathy and compassion to create a peaceful environment can change your perspective and your life experience.

Sure, there's a huge benefit to learning no-nonsense moves designed for street self-defense, but I also show my students how to diffuse fear before it sparks. Dismantling negative emotions by questioning them before they snowball takes away their power to ignite destructive behavior. Are you really in danger? Is this person an actual threat or are your biases making it seem that way? Are you being driven to react by your ego? Can simply allowing the moment to pass resolve the situation?

Once your fear is proven irrational, you can respond appropriately to the moment without being afraid. If your analysis finds that your fear is justified, your response will be different but still appropriate. You may still be afraid, but you'll need to act.

Through practice, your response times will get shorter as you become adept at recognizing the veracity of your emotions. Eventually, the process of questioning your thoughts will feel natural.

A proactive approach to self-protection will help you regain your power, conquer your fear, and reclaim your life:

- » Acknowledge your fear. Give yourself permission to be afraid so you can confront your feelings.
- » Understand your fear. Is it rational? Are you reacting to the past or the present?

- Refocus your fear. Shift it from a problem to a solution. Harness fear's power for fuel.
- Transform your fear. Turn a negative feeling into excitement and confidence.
- Diffuse your fear. When the danger has passed, allow the feeling to pass with it.

The Anatomy of Violence

Some people have never experienced real violence, but their constant diet of fear through the things they watch and listen to can have them on high alert all the time. They are experiencing violence vicariously.

While they may feel they're being practical and educating themselves, simply repeating that crime stats are up or that people get assaulted on the subway doesn't prepare you for actual violence.

Violence isn't pretty. Violence isn't neatly packaged in sixty-second sound bites. Real violence is shocking and explosive. Real violence happens fast but is often the result of pressure that has built up over time — compressed until destructively being released unto the world. While fighters in a ring may artistically set up their attacks, there's no time for fancy traps when a dispute turns physical in real life. You have to keep things simple. A couple of basic techniques that your body can execute quickly can make all the difference.

You don't have to be a super athlete to defend yourself — although being physically fit is definitely an advantage. More importantly, you have to pay attention. Your main weapons are awareness and the willingness to act. The strength and stamina to make it through a fight is important, but the common sense to avoid danger can be more helpful. A healthy lifestyle helps support a powerful body that can protect itself, but a trained mind will spot trouble before it gets too close.

From a practical point of view, it's important to train oneself to maintain a strong, balanced posture, whether sitting or standing. It's a good idea to have a view of exits and entrances when indoors. In a public place, sit facing the front door to ensure you always know who's coming in and out. Early identification of a threat may help you avoid a potentially violent situation.

That doesn't mean you should walk around with balled up fists. You should be relaxed in the moments when there's no reason for tension. Being aware of the worst possible scenario prepares you to deal with whatever comes your way, but this shouldn't come at the expense of a generally peaceful state.

Being relaxed results in quicker action. The less tension you carry, the faster you can respond, and the more likely you are to read a situation appropriately.

Listen to your instincts if something is telling you to be more vigilant. Awareness isn't just useful in avoiding threats, but in recognizing opportunities. If your gut is telling you to pay more attention, you can look at it as a chance to notice something you would have missed, whether it's good or bad. Your gut has neurons and neurotransmitters for a reason. Listen to what it has to say.

You also have to make room for your biases. Your preconceived notions about a person based on their form of dress, race, sex, or religion can contribute to making you feel uneasy or distrustful.

Observing these feelings in ourselves can lead to valuable self-discovery, helping us overcome prejudices that may be hindering social connectivity and overall growth.

Key Takeaways

1 Awareness isn't just for seeing danger, but also for recognizing possibilities.

2 Don't resist the flow of things.

3 Work to control your own fear, and your perception of the world will change.

CHAPTER 4
(Not) Reacting

One of the great things about jiu jitsu is the inclusivity across cultures, races, colors, and creeds. This is partially because of the social network developed in training. That connection allows the practitioner to see all her partners solely as friends and fellow jiujiteiros (Brazilian Portuguese term for jiu jitsu practitioners).

But not everyone is a friend away from the academy. Recognizing potential issues early is your best defense. If a problem can be avoided by crossing the street, it's probably better to cross the street. If someone desperately needs to be told that they're right and you're wrong in order to make their day livable, that's okay.

The more you can let your ego take a bump or two for the greater good, the less defensive you'll be in every interaction, and the less you'll feel attacked.

"Yeah, but, they'll think that I'm . . ."

What? Weak? Are you? That's really for you to decide. Unless your professional reputation is at stake, what does it hurt to acquiesce? To surrender doesn't always mean to quit.

Sometimes surrender means not fighting the inevitable, but embracing it, and using it to your advantage. To ride the wave. To go with the flow.

I can't tell you how many times working in the nightclub business some drunk challenged me to a fight or said he was gonna kick my ass outside the club. They were usually complaining because of the drink I did or didn't serve them, or whether I let them in the club without waiting in line. Sometimes it was because I asked them to follow a rule. None of the reasons were justification to get physical.

I'd have bouncers begging me not to fight. Despite the insults, I walked away nearly every time. As much as I'd want to beat the guy up, I knew it was my ego — not my rational mind — talking. The winner of the brawl could still end up in the hospital, or in jail. That's not much of a win.

But I know even those moments when I didn't walk away were avoidable. I could have let things go or chosen a different perspective. But my ego felt threatened, and I reacted. I wasn't strong enough — didn't have enough control — to stifle my more primal instincts. I wasn't fully domesticated.

Taming that part of me took years of practice. Learning not to judge everything as an attack was a gradual process. There's still an instant internal defensiveness that happens, but I quickly talk myself out of the need to fight, whether in a verbal argument or a physical confrontation.

Avoiding a fight because your cool mind prevailed is a sign of strength. The discipline to control your emotions doesn't always come naturally. Sometimes it takes time and wisdom to realize what's worth fighting for.

Pay It Forward

Conflict is resistance to the flow of things as one force tries to overpower the other to enforce its will. Each puts up a fight because it feels it has to. Moving with the energy being offered by the force that opposes you, like the shoulder rolls of boxer Floyd Mayweather Jr., can help you avoid the hard shots — or at least give time for the full power of a blow to dissipate before reaching you.

Used properly, the energy of your attacker can provide you with the momentum to launch your own counterattack, or to propel you away from the danger. A full-on frontal assault can leave your opponent tired and off balance or be so explosive that it pushes you far away from their gravitational pull.

Whatever the details, the real source of conflict is usually straightforward — people just want to be acknowledged, heard, and valued. Even in a prize fight, that's what the combatants are after. They want to be seen.

Methods for doing this in everyday life vary from artistic expression to bullying. When someone isn't feeling heard, emotions will be expressed or repressed until manifesting as art, a destructive outburst, or a physical ailment.

Hearing someone out, and letting them know their opinion matters, can go a long way to calming egos and avoiding escalation. Boosting someone's self-esteem is free and could be contagious. You could affect a whole bunch of people with one positive comment.

Even in a cage war for the ages, two evenly matched fighters will often feel satisfied regardless of the judges' decision. They have both been completely heard. Both expressed themselves openly and honestly, without the static of the mind. They are at peace at the moment that closing bell rings, when they embrace and thank each other for the transcendent experience that neither could have had on their own.

They were able to momentarily forget their personas and allow consciousness to speak through their instruments — because of the hard work they put in beforehand. They perfectly combined mind, body, and spirit.

This is our ultimate goal and achievement as human beings. To use all we've been given to be all we can be. Great achievement by anyone inspires and is therefore good for all, not just for the participants. It pays itself forward to all who observe it or know of it.

Our constant fear of annihilation, of non-existence from what we perceive existence to be, drives our need to be seen and heard — and simultaneously our dread of being singled out and ostracized.

We want to be acknowledged as individuals, while being accepted as part of a tribe. This can make genuine communication difficult, leading to unnecessary conflict.

Everyone assumes that if there is less conflict, then there is less fear, but it would feel better in reverse.

Less fear, less perceived conflict. Stop resisting the inevitable and the conflict disappears. Stop fighting reality. Control what you can control. Control your own self-generated fear.

When we're shaken by that fear, keeping our balance becomes most important. We may sway side to side or back and forth, but we can't overcommit ourselves in any one direction until we know the threat is real.

Key Takeaways

1 The less tension you carry, the more you can enjoy every moment as it comes, instead of always projecting out into a stressful version of the imaginary future.

2 Hearing someone out, and letting them know their opinion matters, can go a long way to calming egos and avoiding escalation.

3 Great achievement inspires and pays itself forward.

CHAPTER 5
The Standing Dance

There's an exercise I like to do with all my new jiu jitsu students. On day one, when I'm explaining the art to them, we do the push game. It's something my own sensei demonstrated at a seminar he held at my academy years ago. In a minute or so, the push game lets people feel what jiu jitsu is.

The game is simple. My student stands with their feet square and allows me to gently push them off balance. They must step back to regain their equilibrium. After the second or third time, they lean into the push in anticipation. The fourth time, I only pretend to push, and my student has to step forward to keep themselves from falling into me. I move them without laying a finger on them. Their anticipation does them in. They provide the energy for me to pull them forward. This is the essence of jiu jitsu.

> Try the push game for yourself with your sparring partner or someone you trust.

Modern jiu jitsu focuses on ground fighting, but almost all altercations start standing. A de-emphasis on throwing techniques put the Brazilian jiu jitsu (BJJ) fighter at a disadvantage for a long time. Judo slowly became less of a part of BJJ.

There's a certain awkward instability when someone isn't comfortable grappling while standing. The fear is palpable, because if they aren't good at throwing, then they probably aren't good at falling.

The prospect can be terrifying, and the experience can be unpleasant. I once made a classmate throw up from a throw.

But knowing how to take an opponent down is essential to eventually controlling them on the ground. Jiu jitsu fighters without a stand-up game are at the mercy of their opponent in deciding where the fight goes.

> Recent champions have shored up their stand-up skills by incorporating more wrestling and judo into their training, which has made for more complete jiu jitsu fighters.

The stand-up game is largely about timing and rhythm. How an opponent steps, and how you respond, will dictate where their body weight is distributed. Opportunities to throw or take a partner down are created when they are off balance. Making an opponent step into a bad angle just as you attack will have them doing half the work for you.

A stand-up battle that is rhythmless is a horror to watch. Jiu jitsu fighters who are bad at or afraid of standing up will often simply sit down (pull guard) and begin the fight from that position. Of course, this would not be advisable in a street fight.

In judo, where a pin can win a match, athletes stuck on the bottom will sometimes submit rather than attempting to get out. They freeze the game by giving up instead of keeping the give and take going. Any attempt would be better than none. They've stopped the flow before its time.

In relationships, there is always give and take. A dance duo often has a leader, but both partners contribute their own movement to the dance. One steps forward and the other back. One left and the other right.

Traffic flows on either side of the yellow lines in opposite directions. Pistons move machinery. Ships pass in the night. Everything dances.

Chapter 5: The Standing Dance

In an argument, one side pushes while the other pushes back. In a discussion, one side pushes while the other gives way enough to digest new information. It can't be all pushing if anything is to get done — unless everything is to be a war of attrition.

Give and take jiu jitsu requires giving way enough to register what your opponent is doing. Are they really pushing you, or are you being baited? Is their back really that exposed, or are they tricking you into leaving your arm out in the open? If I make him think I'm pulling him, will he pull me back?

The need for rhythm is even more obvious in striking. As a part of traditional Japanese jiu jitsu, effective punches and kicks require setups to be executed properly. Pulling off the setups requires rhythm. Tripping over yourself will lead to being off balance. Your footwork will get you in and out of range. You'll be able to angle out and avoid punches. You need to time when your opponent is moving away or toward you. Footwork produces openings for your shots. You have to calculate just when they'll move their head and in what direction. And you have to do it all while throwing your whole body into your strikes.

If you don't view life as a dance, it just becomes an awkward plodding through existence. When life pushes, you push back. When it pulls, you pull with all your might. And you wonder why nothing is getting done, or you feel like you're losing every time. What chance do you have?

Instead, when our partner steps forward, we should step back — we allow them to come to us, and we're prepared for an attack from that position. If not for the give and take, victory won't come.

Playing to the rhythm of the fight, not against it, allows us to see and feel openings as soon as they happen by noticing disruptions in that rhythm. Beating someone to the punch, throw, or submission means having a split-second advantage. Shortening or lengthening the intervals between the steps of the dance leaves space for offense. Like the silent moment between musical notes, the time in between, the transition, is crucial to the composition.

Key Takeaways

1 Everything is a dance.

2 There has to be give and take for anything to get done.

3 Let your feet move you out of danger and you won't have to fear danger.

CHAPTER 6
Transitions

Nothing stays the same. Everything evolves from something else, eventually deteriorating and beginning the cycle again.

But it's not the end result of the change that is most miraculous, it's the time in between, when the change is actually happening. The often imperceptible, incremental alterations that lead to change are the only difference between our world and a world of still photographs.

In jiu jitsu, true mastery is shown in the transitions — the moments between the photographic stills that lead to optimal positioning. That's when improvisation takes over. When one path closes, another is immediately waiting to be exploited.

Transitions are key because they offer the opponent a moment of freedom from being controlled. To transition, you have to move. Any movement opens up the potential for escape.

When we're frozen by depression or anxiety, there's no transition because there's no movement. Hence, the feeling of being trapped and helpless. Often, it only takes moving a hip to create some space, but when you're being smothered, it's hard to think clearly.

Transitions in jiu jitsu can be from one position of control to another, like a side pin (side control) to a fully mounted position. A transition can also be from submission to submission, gracefully flowing from attack to attack — like going from a rear naked choke to an arm lock.

In our everyday lives, we have no choice but to transition from stage to stage. From the beginning, even just with aging, we're constantly changing. Our choice is either to go with the change and accept it or fight the inevitable with all our might.

Staleness in Stillness

The ugliest thing in jiu jitsu is two super heavyweights doing bad judo. Their goals are always: first, to not get taken down, and second, to not collapse from exhaustion. There are minimal attempts at offense and a ton of stalling. Both combatants are only resisting. There is no dance between forward and back. There is a stale stillness.

These behemoths don't make it into a transition. They stop each other's progress before any of the beauty of the throw can be observed. Or they stand in a posture that would make transitioning to offense nearly impossible.

On the ground, a lot of big guys generally do the same. They lie on their opponent and don't move much. There are few transitions, and little excitement.

Transitions are where the excitement is. Staying stuck to a particular style or ideology only keeps you from transitioning to the next level of your game. It keeps you heavy and bogged down.

Life offers change constantly, and no moment is safe. In fact, each moment has no shot to survive. Everything is transitory. Absolutely nothing is permanent. Even the moment is an illusion, never really existing, because it's gone as soon as it happens, like particles popping into being and vanishing in a flash.

That can be a bummer or a relief, depending on which stage your life is in at the time. In some cases, you don't want to think about the good times ending. In other cases, time can't pass fast enough.

In the transitions, you readjust your route with every new blockade. You foresee obstacles. You realize when it's your time to suffer before you rise again. You appreciate the good times because you remember the bad. You recall when you've fallen into dangerous traps. You work to avoid them.

Transitions from good to bad are just change. There is no stopping change, and it makes for some exciting jiu jitsu.

There's a time between when you trip and when you hit the ground that your body can react in a number of ways. If you've trained, you might go into a shoulder roll or do a proper front fall. If you're untrained, you'll likely fall on your face, hurt your wrists trying to break your fall, or hit your head. I've had several students save themselves because they knew how to fall correctly. It happened to me when I took a spill off a bike and rolled to my feet without thinking about it.

Without action during that trip from the ground to the floor, there is no chance to land safely (or gracefully). You have to be prepared for an eventual fall. Don't look forward to it, but be prepared as if it's inevitable. Then you'll be ready to spin in midair and save yourself.

Key Takeaways

1 Change is inevitable.

2 The beauty of jiu jitsu is in the transitions.

3 Action is necessary to create exciting changes.

4 Be prepared to fall but prepare to save yourself.

SECTION 2: TRAINING YOUR TRAUMA

"Physical self-awareness is the first step in releasing the tyranny of the past."

— Bessel van der Kolk, *The Body Keeps the Score*

CHAPTER 7
Jiu Jitsu Your Life

Communication may not be first on your list of abilities a great fighter needs, but it's essential. A fighter like UFC champion Rose Namajunas has to be a great listener. She must listen honestly but respond dishonestly. Even more importantly she must listen to what's beneath the surface, because her opponents will be lying to her — if they know what they're doing. That's what fakes and feints are about — tricking your adversary.

> You need to listen with a finely tuned body and a clear mind.

Your ego isn't capable of this kind of attuned listening. It plays defense, ensuring your survival by blocking out good and bad or by violently attacking in the hope of staving off any image-shattering information. You're just trying to keep what you have while missing out on what you could be learning. In an attempt to save your persona — but in a primal sense, to save your life — you fight to stay alive.

When you feel emotion well up and threaten to express itself in words, you have to be mindful of what you say. It won't be you talking, and whatever you say will probably mess things up further. What you say in that state may be true, but it almost never turns out to be the best way to solve your problem. Turn off your autoresponder.

Listening lets you craft a reply with your desired solution in mind. Regardless of your response, it's rooted in and relevant to the moment. The alternative is to answer as the person you were in a past experience. But you're not that person anymore. Life has happened, and if you're stuck in the past, then what's the point of all the experience you've gained since then?

Unless it's your goal to live a *Groundhog Day* kind of life, doing and feeling the same things every day, you need to be present in order to take control. You have to feel which way you're drifting from moment to moment to know what direction to steer the wheel. The goal shouldn't be to react before you feel the push or pull which will give you momentum. Guessing might get you there, but anyone can leave life up to chance and just hope for the best. Why not tip the odds in your favor?

The Bumper Car Theory

You learn a lot about a person on the martial arts mat. The same can be said for the bumper car track. The object of the game is to get around the track while harmlessly bumping into other cars. You're in control of the car one moment and careening into a wall the next. This happens whether you try or not, and it can be pretty jarring when you get hit hard.

While it's fun to playfully bump into a friend as you both round the track, there are some people who get downright sadistic. You've seen them. They'll ram random strangers — men, women, and children — with each turn. It's why they got in line for the ride to begin with. They wanted to make some people's brains shake from a sucker punch bumper attack.

But the fun thing about bumper cars is that the little jolts you feel on the way around are enough to wake you up without any real risk. It's not supposed to be unpleasant. Once it gets more real than that, some people get uncomfortable. Others crave that rush.

Light bumpers have fun while letting other people do the same. They can still be aggressive but don't have to T-bone cars driven by five-year-olds to have a good time or feel like they are winning at something that's just supposed to be a fun game for everyone.

In jiu jitsu, hard training against a skilled opponent can be great fun, especially when it feels like a back-and-forth, life-and-death battle. But when the skill level is uneven and one person batters the other, it ceases to be fun for half of the participants. Bumper car hunters are only out for themselves. They don't give a shit about anyone else on the track.

You have to own what kind of driver you want to be. In jiu jitsu, this becomes easy as you progress. Eventually, you're one of the best in class, essentially with superpowers that could render a newbie helpless.

Some people choose the dark side, earning their stripes by bullying the lesser-skilled students. The ones who have been learning the internal principles of jiu jitsu try to make everyone around them better, from white belt to black. They train beginners to eventually surpass them, prepping their own replacement in the pecking order. It's a humbling experience that takes you on an emotional journey which leaves your ego in picces.

Kuzushi

Things you get without resistance are inconsequential. They won't lead to a massive result. They can't. There is no momentum to work with. Often, the catalyst for progress is not a full-frontal assault, but the accumulation of many small steps. These will keep your opponent off balance as you set up the real attack with a fake — a little white lie that will get things moving the way you want them.

Professor Jigoro Kano emphasized kuzushi, the Japanese term for the off-balancing of an opponent. His principles revolutionized martial arts and laid the groundwork for modern interpretations of jiu jitsu. Pushing or pulling an opponent causes them to counter in the opposite direction. When they do, you switch course and take them where they have insisted on going.

Either from within or without, obstacles will appear. They're supposed to. Whether they shove you backwards or pull you into the dark, they provide valuable energy that keeps you moving and can potentially get you where you want to go — if you take control. Kuzushi is cunningly coerced — a gentle manipulation that leads to a dramatic result. Outsmarting the enemy takes far less out of you than going blow for blow. Kuzushi is a way of making life do some of the work for you.

The Pause

You can't be too overzealous with kuzushi. It's about timing and feel. If you're a split second late, your opponent will have settled back into the ground. Too soon and their weight hasn't shifted enough to render them defenseless. It has to be just right.

That's the pause. It's the moment between your fake and real attacks. The tiny window you have to judge your foe's reaction to your offering. If you don't give them a chance to react, then you'll be throwing out one attack after the other, wondering why nothing seems to be working.

A lot of people are good at starting projects, but better at quitting too soon to judge life's reactions to their work. It's not the finished product, but the process involved in getting there that's both the test and the prize. The work is the reward. The results you see are simply the universe's reaction to what you've offered up.

The beauty of jiu jitsu is that its principles carry on through everything you do. Your actions set off a ripple effect that makes things happen. The reverberation of energy produced from deliberate practice builds a bridge between imagination and manifestation, turning fantasy into reality through focused intent. By implementing these principles into your daily practice, you will condition yourself to flow better with what life offers, giving way when necessary, angling out to go around obstacles, and riding fear to victory.

Key Takeaways

1 Anticipating negative events can send us into a spiral of wrong action.

2 Communicating with an opponent is as important as communicating with a friend.

3 If you autorespond, then you're not thinking through your answers.

4 Training should be for the mutual benefit of both practitioners.

5 There's great power in kuzushi (off-balancing).

6 Pausing until the right moment of attack requires patience and discipline.

CHAPTER 8
Trauma and the Kung Fu Master

I once had a lucid dream that I was running down a hallway in my martial arts kimono (also called a gi). As I ran, I knew there was someone around the corner waiting to attack me. Sure enough, when I turned to my right, my top student was waiting. Before I could say anything, he plunged a knife into my gut, and it felt as if it was my destiny to die at his hands.

The dream reminded me of the old Kung Fu Theater movies that aired at 3pm every Saturday when I was a boy. Martial arts were mystical in the 80s. I was a huge buff as a kid, though I never asked my parents for lessons. I did buy a white gi though. And some kung fu slippers, of course.

The first martial artist I ever knew was a tall, half Puerto Rican neighbor I'll call Big A. Always dressed in head to toe black, skull covered by a beret, he was our unofficial security in a building that was anything but secure. As bad as it was, it would have been worse without Big A standing out front all day long, loitering. Without him guarding the gate, there would have been crack deals happening in the vestibule.

His son, Little A, was my best buddy. We'd play in our Justice League Underoos or pretend to be Luke Skywalker and Darth Vader. The aura surrounding his dad was huge. Everyone was slightly scared of Big A, and not just because he was supposed to be a kung fu master. He said he was a Vietnam veteran, but we weren't sure if he was making it up. Big A was known to have a history of mental illness. Everyone thought he could snap at any moment — mostly because he liked it that way. Big A wanted people to be afraid of him.

One day Big A took his volunteer position too seriously. He tried to eject a woman he thought was a prostitute from the front of the building, but her male friend didn't take kindly to the assertion that the young lady was a sex worker. I heard the commotion and ran over to our first-floor apartment's window right next to the front door.

I got to the window just in time to see the entire physical altercation. The much smaller man shoved Big A, who was standing on the top step of our front stoop.

As soon as Big A's back hit the black steel fence that protected the front door, he reached into his back pocket and flicked open a blade so fast that it just looked like he threw a punch. The knife pierced the smaller man's torso. He fell to the dirty cement floor littered with cigarettes and spilled beer. The woman screamed, and Big A bolted upstairs to barricade himself in his apartment.

I was around eight years old. Sometimes I wonder if that's why I became a martial arts instructor. I know it's one of the reasons I lived in fear all my life. Big A never did time. I had to see him every day and think about the smaller man whose life he took. It made me shudder. I knew what he was capable of. I'd known the killer as long as I could remember, I admired him. I thought of him as a kind of eccentric superhero, and he was my best friend's dad to boot. I felt like I had some protection.

But that hero turned into the worst kind of evil. He was responsible for draining the life from the eyes I tried to peer into from my window. And Big A didn't bat an eye. It was as if it never happened. As if I hadn't seen what I had seen. There was no remorse. I lost a best friend and a big piece of my childhood when I watched that man die.

Chapter 8: Trauma and the Kung Fu Master

Taking the Trauma with You

That day I learned that human life doesn't mean the same thing to everyone. Some people discount the value of another soul, living for themselves — driven by their animal instincts. Suddenly, the fights I saw everyday could be death matches. I was terrified.

The relief after moving away from that neighborhood eight years later was like a release valve opening. I didn't have to worry about looking someone in the eye for too long or dodging the drug dealers on the block. There were no more guns being put to my head or junior high school gang fights. I could relax now.

Yeah, right.

Getting your body to let go of trauma that's locked in at an early age can be a lifelong struggle. While many of us try to shrug off our past by blocking out mental images, it's our physical self that holds on to the memories. You don't need conscious thoughts to put you back in that traumatic time and place. A subconscious reminder is reason enough for your body to freak out as it tries to protect you.

Thanks to reduced stigma, partially because of the prevalence of mental health issues, greater access to information, and books like *Your Body Keeps the Score* by Bessel van der Kolk, more people are understanding how triggers can manifest into physical symptoms and spiraling thoughts. The separation of body and mind that happens in the midst of trauma leaves the trembling body alone and unprotected in an attempt to barricade the fragile mind.

But that body doesn't forget the event that the rational mind was absent for. Our ability to dissociate comes at a huge cost. There are no free rides. You don't escape the trauma because you don't think about it.

So, treating the physical body as well as the mind becomes crucial. Retraining yourself not to react to certain stimuli isn't easy. For me, it was akin to training a wild dog to sit and obey. Forcing myself to meditate, as difficult as it was at the beginning, started to give me more control of my physical and emotional reactions. Each time I growled, I lightly pulled my own leash — compassionately, but with authority.

The rational mind must become the boss of the body. If the body is left to take control, you can be transported to the worst time of your life, or driven to destructive behavior. In recovering from trauma, a new type of discipline is born. Dominion over your physical reactions can thwart negative thoughts before they have a chance to fester.

After more than two decades practicing martial arts, I know that mastering fighting doesn't make you superhuman or take away your fear. Then again, I really learned that lesson forty years ago, when I saw the giant, scared kung fu master pull fear from his back pocket. That's when I stopped believing in superheroes.

Key Takeaways

1 One traumatic moment can stick with you for your entire life.

2 Emotions get trapped in the body, causing a thought and feeling loop that keeps you stuck.

3 The rational mind must become the boss of the traumatized body.

CHAPTER 9
Self-Defense vs. Self-Empowerment

Long after I knew how to fight, I was still scared. I was an expert in hand-to-hand combat, standing up and on the ground. I grew up on the rough side of town. I knew what real violence was like.

But it still terrified me. The thought that something could happen at any moment had me on edge. I'd expect people to start trouble with me. I was looking for it, because I was afraid. No amount of physical training took that fear away. It was locked up tight, constricted in the tiny body of an eight-year-old me. The fear had settled in and was petrified. So, as the outer shell became impenetrable, the center trembled.

That unending fear brought shame. I thought I was a coward for being afraid, even though I never showed it. I still got angry, and fought when I had to, but it was all out of fear.

Hard training brought temporary relief. Intense battle makes you forget everything, including fear. Fighting puts you in the present. Fear is always somewhere else.

But after the adrenaline was gone and the aches and pains began, the fear would return. I'd feel weak again.

I had a black belt teammate who would have to take copious amounts of anxiety medication before training because he was so terrified of failing. During sparring, he was zoned in and looking to take one of your limbs home with him. Other times of the day, he was a powder keg, jumping out of his skin, with a mind that bounced around faster than the speed of light.

All the preparation in the world won't take away a threat that's coming from a place you can't see or just choose not to address. That stored fear will be seething just under the surface.

For self-defense to become self-empowerment, you need to cultivate awareness of your own reactions and responses to stress and perceived danger and where those reactions come from. Being armed with this information can diffuse potential confrontations in your mind before they materialize.

You'll quickly reevaluate a thought or feeling for its validity when cross-referenced against your biases and preconceptions. A split-second decision can make the difference between the right choice and tragedy.

The ability to assess situations preemptively will fill you with confidence. You won't live in fear based on the past or perceived future.

Taking Power Back

Self-empowerment enhances your life by alleviating triggers through a deeper understanding of human behavior and archetypes. The hothead, the blowhard, the narcissist, the hero, the white knight, or the complainer are all out there. And no matter where you go, one of them will show up.

Understanding your own thoughts and feelings — and being able to empathize with others — goes a long way toward reducing fear and disdain. It's the unknown, or the qualities we dislike in ourselves, that are so scary.

Seeing threats where there are none is a paralyzing predicament. You should be aware of your surroundings without being afraid of them. Knowing why people tend to get defensive, how someone else's fear can come off as aggression, how appearance is not always what it seems, and how we can choose to react differently to perceived slights can serve as early warning signs designed to shut down the potential for a violent altercation.

Chapter 9: Self-Defense vs. Self-Empowerment

There are lots of tough guys out there who are also scared all the time. Some of them become bullies. I never went that route. Instead, I beat myself up for not being tougher, while everyone around me thought I was a badass.

It wasn't until I got in touch with the lingering fear inside me and acknowledged it without judgment that my fear of the outside world dissipated. My heart no longer raced when I sensed trouble. Instead, there was a type of "spidey sense" that gave me a little tingle — reminding me to be more aware. Without the anxiety of fear, I became confident in my training, because I knew I was relaxed enough to execute techniques if I had to protect myself — or someone else.

Without the confidence of having sparred and pressure tested your martial art, you won't know if it works at all. And while you live in fear, you'll be too stiff to perform the movements effectively in a real situation, so you won't be as confident.

I'd bet on a fully realized, self-aware person being far less likely to get into a fight than a well-trained, emotionally stunted, severely traumatized brute with low self-esteem. Fear can smell fear. It seeks it out.

No one is completely free of fear, but fear based on a real impending threat is far different than manufactured fear. I firmly believe that everyone should learn the basics of fighting, but only as an overall approach to self-empowerment. Don't let a misunderstanding turn into a fight, a broken hand, busted nose, or a night in jail. Use your first layer of empowerment — awareness — before you go kicking someone in the groin because they tried asking you for directions.

Key Takeaways

1 Fear can cause shame.

2 Living in fear keeps you on edge.

3 Acknowledging fear helps overcome it.

4 Understand your reactions, as well as what others may perceive as dangerous.

CHAPTER 10
Confidence and Combat Sports

Self-defense skills and the confidence they instill are meant to free you to live your life without constant fear. Would you be safer locked in your home all day? Sure, but once you've binge-watched everything on Netflix or run out of toilet paper you'll have to face the world.

Empowerment is freedom. Freedom to go to more places and do more things, but also freedom from the debilitating feelings of stress and anxiety that come from low self-confidence.

That freedom isn't just going to allow you to walk down a dark street you might otherwise avoid, but it's going to help you talk to that classmate you've been wanting to chat with. It's going to help you ask your boss if you can run some ideas by them. It will help you stand up for yourself at home or at work.

And that should be the case with any training program or discipline you undertake. The point isn't just to punch or kick, or to have visible abs, or even to fight off some drunk. The point of training is to make every part of your life better. Discipline is infectious, spreading from one section of your being to the next. Commitment to any training is commitment to making yourself better at everything you do, if even in the most negligible way. Among my favorite alternatives to martial arts training are:

- Hot yoga
- Bike rides
- Bodywork such as focused stretching, massage, or breaking up scar tissue for recovery

- Light kettlebell workouts
- Watching videos of matches or fights to keep techniques fresh in your mind
- Writing out sequences that you can imagine performing, with as much detail as possible

The discipline to train yourself to act leads to the discipline to not act when inaction is a better alternative. The ego can never be the decider of this, because it will risk your life to save its own. Your ego might have you mouth off to an agitated, mentally unstable man who is holding up the train doors. It'll let you deal with the repercussions.

Beating the Ego

Overriding the ego can help prevent most conflicts. You must ignore the jealous little voice in you that always thinks it's being disrespected, the one that always feels so small that it has to constantly prove itself. It needs to be acknowledged to know it's not in danger of being destroyed. If you confuse its voice with your own, then you'll act out of fear and survival. You'll need to posture, and you'll miss out on genuine interaction.

Your ego needs to be reconditioned, like a bratty child. Habit and family dynamic may have made the ego leery of sharing and quick to lash out when it doesn't get its way.

When you sense judgment in yourself, immediately address it. Ask yourself where it's coming from, and why you feel the need to judge this aspect of a particular person. What is it about you that has made you focus on this flaw in them?

As you see the perceived weakness in yourself, you'll begin to see the origins of the disdain you feel for others — the ways they remind you of you. That leaves you with the option of either hating yourself and everyone else, or finding compassion for your faults and theirs.

Smart Hulk

All real heroes have sidekicks. Even Superman had Lois Lane helping him out, and eventually the Justice League. In some ways, we act like the sidekick who turns to the hero to lead the way and provide strength in times of difficulty, because we don't feel worthy of being the hero ourselves.

I prefer to think of myself more like Smart Hulk from the "Avengers" films. Now, I know that may sound a bit egotistical — but hear me out.

Smart Hulk found a way to integrate the shadow part of his personality — his anger, rage, and overwhelming power — into his thinking side — Dr. Banner. The result is an unstoppable combination. Once he gave up fighting the Hulk side of himself, which he couldn't kill without killing himself, he came to terms with who he was as a whole and what he was truly capable of.

I've come to terms with the idea that both parts of my personality can exist together. Bruce Banner thought he could only be the green monster or the brilliant scientist, but not both at once. He feared his powerful alter ego.

Early on, I thought I had to play up the meathead portion of me to protect myself. My intellectual side sat on the sidelines while I built a tough exterior. Reconciling those two poles are what have allowed me to come closer to my true self.

All the ideas in the world will do you no good without the fire to implement them. It takes far more to make things happen.

Poet, painter, and philosopher, William Blake said we all gain wisdom from heaven and power from hell.[5] We are connected to both and capable of great levels of good and evil. The power to defend oneself and others effectively and intelligently requires a realization of Blake's philosophy. While our intentions may be righteous, our actions must sometimes be violent.

If you're an expert grappler, you may not cause any harm at all. You could simply control your opponent, or use your skills to evade and get away, or maybe you just do a marginal amount of actual bodily harm. But you must be willing to hurt someone when you act, because a lesser level of intensity will likely lead to complete failure.

If you're training for self-defense and pretending it will be neat and clean, then you're deluding yourself. Maybe that's what you're after. Or all you need.

Maybe, like the blue marble flying and spinning through space at 1,000 mph, you need to pretend you're standing still to feel okay with it all.

It's understandable. If you think about it too hard, it can be scary — or liberating. To know that in the grand scheme, things really aren't much in our control. We need to do something to help us pretend to be safer. We need to be safer in our minds, like a self-defense placebo.

Placebos work. If you're taking a capoeira class, and you feel like a badass but are still a nice person, then awesome! If you are holding your head up high because of your cardio kickboxing class, or Pilates, or whatever makes you feel like the strong person you are capable of being, great!

Keep it going. Never stop. If you do stop, then find something else right away. Do things that make you feel confident, powerful, and safe, because feeling is everything.

Key Takeaways

1 Knowing you have a chance of defending yourself builds confidence.

2 Controlling your ego will keep you out of trouble.

3 There's a voice that tells you not to quit. Listen.

4 Be willing to tap into your dark side to defend yourself.

SECTION 3: FINDING THE RIGHT ANGLE

"Never forget: This very moment, we can change our lives. There never was a moment, and never will be, when we are without the power to alter our destiny. This second, we can turn the tables on Resistance."

— Steven Pressfield, *The War of Art*

CHAPTER 11
Judging Books by Their Covers

The best Krav Maga (Israeli self-defense) practitioner I ever met took my class on my last day teaching at a small academy in Brooklyn. Until then, no one who had come through the door impressed me much with their fighting skills. This day was different.

It was common to have Orthodox Jews training in private classes. I had an entire Orthodox family training with me at once — Dad and his four kids. All in their conservative, religious dress, except one rebellious daughter who always sported short shorts, a tube top, and a dozen tattoos and piercings.

When an Orthodox woman walked in on my last day, wearing a long wig and a longer dress, I wasn't surprised. When she started moving, I thought I was dreaming.

This woman moved exactly like me. She matched my rhythm and intensity. She was fast and powerful, smashing through her less skilled training partners. I was amazed. Everyone was. She'd ask about each technique I showed, then performed exactly how I demonstrated — or better. As she flowed from move to move, her seemingly endless dress swayed to and fro. She was gliding like an Orthodox female Jason Bourne, her wig staying perfectly in place. She barely broke a sweat, despite being covered up from head to toe.

I was in awe of this woman. After class, we fawned over each other, both saying how we felt a connection as martial artists that is rare. I lamented that I wouldn't get the chance to teach her again but told her I hoped we'd meet in the future.

> **Big Power in Little Packages**
> Coaches worth anything are always overjoyed to see the practice performed expertly and with grace. I should have known not to judge that woman by her appearance.

One of the toughest bouncers I've ever known was Jimmy V. — Judo Jimmy as they called him. Despite standing at about 5'5", Jimmy was the head bouncer at some huge New York City nightclubs. Jimmy had everyone's respect because they knew his pedigree, and they'd seen what he could do to much bigger people. It didn't matter if you were huge; Jimmy could smash you.

Then there was Evor. This dude was tiny. A multiple-time masters world champion, the Brazilian jiu jitsu black belt Evor made the stocky Judo Jimmy look like the Rock. But Evor was so fast, so flexible, and so skilled, that he'd have you tapping or napping before you knew it.

But the best ego adjuster is when somebody like Ms. Sung gets her hands on you. Ms. Sung probably weighed less than a hundred pounds, but her catlike reflexes and multiple black belts made her a tiger in tabby clothing. She could spin-kick your head off or break your arm — pick your poison. Either way, you'd be defeated.

None of these martial artists could be judged by their appearance, yet their strength, built through years of discipline, shone through more than that of other people. It's their self-assurance from having been tested in a fight that makes them exude a certain confidence, even if they don't consciously feel that way.

There's an air about them — something special about someone who is willing to move close enough to strike and to get hit in order to hit back. Most people who take a hard shot will turn away or take a knee. They'll find a way to quit.

Looking Tough vs. Being Tough

The majority of jiu jitsu practitioners abandon ship after getting a second belt. It's enough for them to see the change from white to blue — a sign of progress in their otherwise static lives. These men and women might be successful off the mat, but they long for something more primal in their time away from the office. Jiu jitsu offers them that escape, if just for a brief time. A chance to prove they can overcome adversity in and out of the academy.

Then there are the grinders — those who sharpen their instruments day in and day out, year after year — until each pendulous swing of their limbs delivers dangerous consequences.

Those precious few don't come in cookie cutter sizes. Society has misjudged what tough is. Since most people haven't been in a fight, or participated in any kind of combat sport, who's dangerous and who isn't is different from the perception of a seasoned martial artist or street fighter. Posture, eye contact, and speech patterns can give away a lot about confidence, which often reflects an ability to let go in a fight.

But there are also fighters who are great in part due to their neurodiversity. There are world class athletes who can focus on their sport at a superhuman, obsessive level. Most of these athletes are not physically imposing, and many even look like the first person a bully would pick on in high school (just look at jiu jitsu world champion Mikey Musumeci).

I took the opposite route. I made myself look big, tough, and scary while I still felt small, frail, and scared as hell. I think that's why I admire these unlikely powerhouses even more. I know what it's like to be a muscle-bound meathead who assumes he can manhandle a skinny guy. I also know that it wasn't until I stripped away most of that muscle that I could toss around giants.

The little guy can win. It takes skill, preparation, and the willingness to get close enough to strike. If you look in the mirror and see someone too small to be lethal, too little to make a dent, too tiny to effect change, don't fret. Be certain that if you learn what you have to learn, do what you know you need to do, and take it as far as you can go, then you'll bring Goliath to his knees.

Key Takeaways

1 Never judge anyone's fighting prowess based on how they look.

2 Recognize your own abilities.

3 Looking tough doesn't mean being tough.

4 The smaller person always has a chance to win.

CHAPTER 12
Rolling through Danger

Belt colors create an interesting hierarchy at martial arts schools. White belts desperately want to be blue belts, so they don't get beaten up anymore. Blue belts want the cache of instructor level with the purple belt. Purple belts can't wait to earn stripes against brown belts. And brown belts are tasting that black belt around the corner. Then the black belts have targets on their backs because everyone thinks they have superpowers.

Beginners want to roll (spar) with us because they want to see how it feels to face their fears and train with a black belt — and some of them enjoy getting mangled. Higher belts want to see if they can test us.

While most of the lower belts won't have a chance against the black belt, if they go in scared, then they've lost already. Psyching yourself out is a real thing. The self-doubt that you can't conquer something will ensure your failure.

It's not that we don't all feel fear, but many of us can also go into stressful situations calm and composed. Danger doesn't enter our thoughts.

The difference is twofold. First, those who train or compete without a sense of danger have done a better job of coming to terms with death. Fear of anything is ultimately fear of death. Fighters often say they are willing to die to win a fight, and they mean it. That type of freedom can turn fear into the willingness to do anything to win.

Second, and most importantly, past trauma can affect how dangerously a situation is viewed. Someone who was smothered in an assault may be sensitive to being trapped under an opponent. Some women are hesitant to train with men, or vice versa, because of incidents of harassment in the past. Training can cause people to recall violent events they've endured.

I had a student who was an ex-soldier. He was deployed in the Middle East during conflict in Afghanistan. Each time he trained on the mat, he had absolutely no control and would often injure his training partners. This man had one speed: Kill. Off the mat, he was the sweetest guy.

When you're programmed to see danger everywhere, it's difficult to decipher friend from foe. With jiu jitsu, every foe is a friend, because each one teaches you about yourself. The sport creates a whole new dynamic between adversaries.

> When danger becomes a game, there is little that can scare you.

Exposing Danger

Sometimes you can sense real danger. Awareness is your number one weapon against it. Avoiding potentially violent situations can only be done when you're awake to your surroundings. A lack of awareness leads to overblown prospects of danger.

Knowing what you're up against always reduces stress. Just as understanding your opponent's repertoire before a match calms your nerves, seeing a potential problem before it approaches allows for the time to avoid a dangerous moment before the threat is already upon you.

A New York City subway platform is a good example. The distance from one end to the other is significant, yet the echo allows for faraway sounds to be heard — but only if you're paying attention. Noise canceling headphones and handheld devices take much of the focus of commuters. There can be a fight brewing a few feet away, and the passengers are clueless until the melee is on top of them.

Jiu jitsu requires seeing danger coming. Often referred to as a human chess match, you have to see several moves in advance while simultaneously remaining in the moment in order to respond appropriately.

Life should be enjoyed, but it still takes focus. Feeling free from danger requires learning about the things that remind your body and mind of real danger you've faced in the past. So much of the danger we perceive is based on fear of future events we only imagine.

The difference between jiu jitsu and some other traditional martial arts is that there is no imagination necessary to know if it works. Everything we practice is tried in live training. And we don't have to live in fear of not knowing if we'll ever be submitted. We will be. And we'll survive.

Key Takeaways

1   Seeing danger where there is none leads to under or overreaction.

2   Your past can dictate what you see as dangerous.

3   Fear of impending danger will make you lose before you begin.

4   Stay aware so you can see threats coming early.

CHAPTER 13
Knowing When to Tap

There are times when there is seemingly no escape. You have exhausted your options, and everything seems hopeless. Without mercy, your fate is sealed.

This is the time to tap. It's the moment when you've given all you have, but still find yourself on the brink of total defeat. On the battlefields of the samurai, that defeat would have meant death. On jiu jitsu mats, it's only admitting that the person you were just training with could have killed you if they wanted to.

That's a tough pill for the ego to swallow. If you were actually dead, then you wouldn't have to live with the shame of having surrendered to another human. To fight valiantly and lose one's life is heroic, but to give in could be seen as cowardice.

The dilemma in jiu jitsu is that to get good, you have to quit a lot in the beginning. You'll have no choice. Unless you want to walk around with dislocated joints, you'll have to tap out.

Giving 100 percent to a battle only to come out on the short end is heartbreaking. Defeat is crushing, and though only your ego is hurt on the mats, it can feel like the world is collapsing in on you in everyday life.

Most of us want to continue the fight no matter what. We don't want to quit because of what it would say about us. We'd rather keep dealing with the pain of doing what's not working, rather than feeling as if we've given up.

I had a student who wouldn't tap to strangulations. He would instead allow himself to be choked unconscious during training. Each time, he would wake up suddenly saying he was okay. It wasn't enough to bring himself to the brink of death, he had to take it further. He had to prove to himself that he wouldn't give up, even if it meant dying.

Being embarrassed by having to acquiesce to an opponent's attack will block your ability to learn from the defeat. You may simply see revenge as your goal, rather than tangible improvement that would prevent the same result next time. Aggression may seem like the answer to best your foe, but this can lead to a quicker defeat.

I always hated tapping. I felt a tremendous pressure to be undefeated on the training mat, and being submitted would lead to sleepless nights. It wasn't until I realized I couldn't always do things on my own, and sometimes I'd have to surrender to something or someone greater than me, that I began to see tapping as an acceptable thing to do.

There's a big difference between being submitted and quitting. An athlete who gives his all in a match but is forced to tap by a superior competitor has no reason to hang his head. Submitting is not surrender due to cowardice. Tapping out means you live to fight another day — and in one piece.

Surrender shouldn't be seen as losing, but as a chance to reset. When life seems to be going all wrong, despite what we do we're sometimes brought to our knees. Continuing to fight from this position of weakness is futile. There's an outside grace that must act to save you.

When it comes to jiu jitsu, that grace comes in the form of a partner who releases the hold that could have caused your demise. In twelve step programs, that grace is given by a higher power. In either case, escaping on your own has become an impossibility.

When you know going in that you'll have to tap multiple times, your stress level is lower. You know you have no chance to defeat your opponent, so you are only there to learn. While you still try your best, the difference in skill is too much to be made up by effort.

Sometimes in life, we're overmatched. Overwhelm strikes us all. Still, we rise every day and take on the challenges of our lives. Those challenges can become so stacked that we're buried under them, punching our hand through the rubble in hopes of being pulled out by someone.

Chapter 13: Knowing When to Tap

That's the time to tap. When you can't get out on your own. When another move on your part may only make things worse. When you're twisted into a pretzel and you can't see a speck of light, stick your hand out and tap. There's no shame in it.

Key Takeaways

1 You won't always be able to escape on your own.

2 Tapping out sometimes is a part of the game.

3 The ego will make you believe surrender is the same as quitting.

4 Submitting to a higher power (or belt) isn't shameful.

CHAPTER 14
Competition and Fear

I used to hate roller coasters. The slow click, click, click to the top terrified me. I always wanted to get off the moment we'd start the ascent. Fear gripped every cell in my body as I prepared my heart for the shock of the fall.

After the first ride of the day, all the other coasters would feel easier. Still, I didn't enjoy the rides much. It was more about the challenge of just getting through it.

It used to be the same for me and competition. I took things so seriously that competing felt like a life-or-death situation. The fear of failure was a desperate red alert that there was danger ahead. I always wanted to back out.

There were times I'd cry before competitions because the feeling of terror made me want to run and hide. Before I had my jiu jitsu school, there was less pressure, but I was still afraid. Back then, I competed to become friends with fear. I figured if I could control the butterflies in my stomach when someone was trying to throw or strangle me, I could control them anytime.

I know the exact day that my fear of competition broke. I was having deep doubts about everything, and even told my wife at the time that I was done with martial arts because I hated it. It was two weeks out from a tournament, and I despised everything about training. I thought if I lost, all my students would think less of me — or worse, they would leave me. Then, it hit me.

The greatest piece of advice my inner voice ever gave me: Nobody cares. Nobody cares if you lose. The people who love you are still going to love you. The haters will still hate. But most people just won't give a shit.

> You're not going to change anyone who matters'
> opinion by winning a gold medal.

Two weeks later I had my best performance to date at a tournament. While I did win the gold, the most important thing was that I had fun during the entire process. From flying out, to watching my teammates and coach compete ahead of me, to the time before my matches, I had a smile on my face. I was so relaxed I took a nap before it was my turn to step on the mat.

That experience showed me it was only my mindset that made me feel anxious and scared before a match. There was nothing wrong with me. I knew from coaching that everyone feels tremendous fear before they fight. The important thing is how that fear is harnessed and interpreted. It was a couple of years before I competed again, and an injury brought more doubt into my mind. I thought that winning the Masters World Championship at my previous tournament meant I couldn't lose, or I'd delegitimize the title I'd won.

While that tournament was horrible from beginning to end, it was again because I was putting tremendous pressure on myself. I lost my first match of that tournament after my knee popped. Although I felt terrible, I got over it and went on to coach my students at the same competition. My team performed great, and none of them thought any less of me for losing.

My next three competitions were a good time from beginning to end. Although I didn't win, I performed well, and I showed my students the most important lesson I wanted them to learn and I needed to remember — it's supposed to be fun, win or lose.

Letting Resistance Stop You

One of the best students I ever had, who struck fear in the hearts of other kids, was deathly afraid to compete. On multiple occasions I had to practically beg him to step on the mat because his anxiety was so bad. He would win every match in spectacular fashion, but he had a horrible fear of letting people down. At one tournament, which he would have dominated, his mom and I pleaded with him not to back out, but he was determined to withdraw.

But I didn't push him anymore once I saw how bad his anxiety was. He had reached a point where getting him to calm down in time for his match would have been impossible.

There's no doubt that if my student had competed, he would have felt a massive sense of accomplishment, or at least would've built up some resilience. Deciding not to compete was a win only for the resistance that tries to bog all of us down.

We can all think back to a time when resistance got the better of us. We felt it blocking our path, and we gave in. The thought of going over or around the obstacle didn't occur to us. The idea that the blockade is meant to redirect us to the right path didn't enter our minds. We took no for an answer.

Like in judo, that "no" is simply the initial reaction of your opponent: resistance. As you push and feel it push back, you can either use its massive power to your advantage, or see it as a foreign invader from which you need to hide.

The voice that resists is inside of you. You can't outrun it, and you shouldn't want to. It tells you what you need to do by the things it tries to keep you away from. It will tell you that you're not good enough, that you'll fail and be humiliated. And humiliation is often perceived as the possibility of being shunned. That potential disconnection is akin to death in the deep recesses of your mind.

> The important thing is how fear is harnessed and interpreted.

Ego Death

Ego death feels no different than the impending doom of legitimate calamity. Our personas are constructed on frail pillars. A threat to a part of who we imagine ourselves to be is a threat to all that we think we are.

"If I am not that," we think, "then I am nothing." The thought of being nothing is too much for some people.

To be nothing is to be empty. When you're empty, there's no baggage to weigh you down. There's room in you for new knowledge and new experiences. There's no doctrine to be upheld or personality to preserve. You're open to change and growth. You aren't trying desperately to hold on to who you are at this moment.

Once I conquered my fear of competition, roller coasters were a cinch. Just like I trained myself to enjoy every part of the experience of competing, I became enamored with every part of a roller coaster ride: the tinge of fear when you first look at the size of the track, the butterflies while waiting in line, getting strapped into the seat, the harness locking in place. There's no backing out. The sound of the horn announces the ride is about to start. Click, click, click, and I'm smiling away — giddy.

Nowadays I ride coasters with my nine-year-old daughter. I've trained her to embrace her fear and go for it anyway. She's a performer, and I've only seen her experience stage fright once. She likes the biggest, scariest coasters and water slides. She's even done trapeze. I think part of her enjoys the fear now. When she feels it, she tells me she knows she has to do the thing to get over being afraid.

I've since graduated from roller coasters to skydiving. Jumping out of a plane was maybe the most peaceful experience I've ever had. I pretended I was an action hero going to save someone. I'm not sure I could've had that experience without the years of doubts and fear I thought would consume me. I had to stop fearing the fall so I could fly.

Chapter 14: Competition and Fear

Key Takeaways

1 The thing you fear the most will bring you the greatest satisfaction if you can conquer it.

2 No one who matters will care if you don't win.

3 Resistance isn't meant to stop you, but to guide you to where you need to be.

4 Fall in love with the process, butterflies and all, and you can have fun from beginning to end.

CHAPTER 15
Butterflies Are Your Friends

Anxiety is energy bound up and in need of focused expression. Needing to move but not knowing where to go, we're left spinning in place. Gyrating and swaying, wanting to go this way and that at once.

Jiu jitsu can't be this way. For a technique to work properly and without the need for additional strength, all of the body's power must be moving against a single limb. Or a body must have the advantage of trickery on its side to make the opponent put himself in danger. Action is calculated. Responses are measured.

Anxiety allows for neither. Calculation is impossible when you're glitching, and any response you give will only be a reaction to whatever trigger sets off your anxiety to begin with.

To direct your energy, you must have a target. While in a match, you may go in with a game plan, but your opponent can throw off your rhythm and ruin your attack. When this happens, a good practitioner adjusts and takes what their partner is giving them. If an arm becomes available, it's quickly snatched up. A neck is wrapped up by an arm. Or a leg becomes tangled in between two legs.

When you're anxious, it's essential to find a goal to apply your overflowing energy to. This allows you to expel nervous tension by doing something pleasant that you're good at, something you can turn to in good times and bad. Being anxious and busy is better than being anxious and bored.

But it's not enough to ward off anxiety after it hits. Understanding the source of your anxious feelings is imperative to preemptively stop debilitating attacks. Through mindfulness — paying close attention to your thoughts, feelings, and actions — you can come to know your anxiety triggers.

If it can be addressed immediately, then do it. But if it's something you need to avoid for a little while until you work up the dexterity to handle it again, there's no shame in that.

Anxiety before training is common in jiu jitsu. Although there shouldn't be the pressure of a competition each time you step on the mat, there often is. For those who normally suffer from anxiety, a trip to the academy can be like tiptoeing through a minefield. Opening oneself up to the humiliation of submission to another human being is humbling enough. Failing in front of your instructor can feel like disappointing your dad.

> **Many practitioners meditate, use visualization, or smoke cannabis before training and competition to relax their anxiety.**

Being calm under pressure when your anxiety should be ramped up is a huge part of what jiu jitsu is about. A good black belt looks very relaxed, no matter how heated the competition gets. While his body is giving its all, his mind must be clear. His physical self must be unimpeded by the feeling of anxiety.

White Belt Scrambles vs. Black Belt Scrambles

In jiu jitsu, there are often scrambles of action that result in the athletes losing and regaining position in rapid succession. Although these scrambles may seem chaotic, when done by skilled practitioners, there's an amazing beauty to the movement and technical prowess involved in flowing from offense to defense and back again.

At the 2024 Craig Jones Invitational tournament, jiu jitsu athletes Kade Ruotolo and Andrew Tackett battled for three five-minute rounds of nonstop action. It was a scramble from beginning to end, and although it didn't end in a submission, the match is widely regarded as one of the greatest of all time. The expertise with which they moved from one position to the next made it artistry. The lack of a finish didn't make the match any less satisfying to watch.

When beginners scramble, it's like two clumsy oafs trying their hardest to hurt each other by any means necessary, and maybe hurt themselves in the process. Arms and legs flailing everywhere, there's nothing artistic about their exchange.

Gaining control over anxiety is growing from the scrambling white belt to the measured black belt. It's focusing all your energy into one place in order to harness your power. It's relaxing in the midst of the chaos and not letting anxious thoughts block your body's potential, or allowing your body's signals to create a mental frenzy.

Transforming the Feeling

My daughter recently had her first piano recital, and I gave her the same advice I give my students when they compete. Relax, have fun, and remember those butterflies are your friends.

Most of the time, the physical feelings we experience before intimidating or challenging situations are interpreted as nervousness, danger, or fear. Instead, those feelings should be viewed on the flip side — excitement. There's no difference between the chemicals released; only your mind's interpretation decides how you translate them. Just watch the people on roller coasters. Same experience — some are terrified while others laugh hysterically.

It's really up to you to choose to turn an event from anxiety or fear to excitement and anticipation. One of the worst parts of anxiety is not knowing what will happen next. What if that were viewed as an adventure? What if we used the extra energy we feel to focus on the moment, and just saw where it took us, without any idea of where that could be?

Jiu jitsu is that way. You begin your match without any real idea where it will end. Even if you're used to a certain opponent, an infinite number of scenarios could occur. Although there are adversaries with whom you'll reach a stalemate because you know each other so well, those are the most boring matches — when you already know how they'll turn out.

Philosophical writer Alan Watts once made the analogy that you don't go to the symphony to hear the final note.[6] The goal isn't to get to the end the fastest. He and others have said a life in which we already know the end is a life not worth living. Anxiety goes against this edict. It's rushing to get nowhere. Hurry without a destination. Madness.

Key Takeaways

1 Energy has to be focused to gain an advantage over an opponent. Anxiety kills focus.

2 Find the source of your anxiety to avoid triggers.

3 Jiu jitsu requires calmness under pressure.

4 Fear and excitement release the same chemicals. Only your mental interpretation decides which you are feeling.

5 A seemingly mad scramble performed with skill can lead to a spectacular victory.

CHAPTER 16
Wanting to Quit

There's a moment in a tough match when you wish you weren't there. You begin to resist the moment, because your discomfort has grown. You're stuck in a bad spot, running out of gas, with no escape in sight.

I could easily be describing the paralysis of deep depression. The heaviness of despair in the midst of an episode is like being pinned on your back by a sumo wrestler. Pushing him away would be useless.

If depression can't be pushed away, can't be forced onto the back burner, then it has to be dealt with. It has to be accepted before being acted upon.

When stifled by a smothering opponent, particularly a larger one, you can only hope to use the adversary as a frame to escape.

Depression is the opponent you are building the frame off of. The emotion has to be grasped with both hands. Hands need to be braced for inward movement but prepared to push — to move while keeping the frame.

That frame is the foundation that holds your structure together, and it must stay firm yet pliable. Strong but soft. Unbreakable, but infinitely bendable.

Depression will stretch you to your maximum. You will struggle from the pressure — heavy on your chest. As your opponent holds you there, you're unable to find a millimeter of space to move, and your world closes in further. You realize your only hope is for them to make a mistake. You're at their mercy in one way, but prepared for opportunity in another.

Will you be ready when you get a tiny opening to break out of the doldrums? We get chances to join in laughter or celebration all the time when we're down, but we don't feel up to taking advantage of it.

What if you fought your instincts and forced your way through the activity? Sure, you might have an anxiety attack, but you might also break through your depression with a smile and a good time. It's been known to happen.

Bad Days Turn Good

On days when you come in feeling tired and kind of off, you often have your best training sessions — likely because your body is more relaxed and less connected to your mind for information. Your body is working off its own ingrained knowledge, so the movement is instant.

When we ruminate, going over our perceived problems again and again, we're frozen by overthinking. Too many options create inaction. New practitioners often inundate their viewing habits with technique videos that increase the repertoire of moves they only vaguely understand and can't yet connect into their games.

Overthinking during training will leave you asleep to what your opponent is doing. You're too immersed in yourself. Unaware of the outside world. Focused on whatever vacuum you may be feeling. Whatever emptiness has left you looking for something.

When you're lost inside yourself, it's easy to miss what's in front of you. Sometimes you might not even take a moment to look up, your eyes fixed on the ground to avoid any direct gazes.

To be good at jiu jitsu, you need to be in touch with your surroundings and your place in them. You can't think of yourself as separate from your opponent, but as one entity moving together, ending with you in an advantageous position.

A depressed person feels stranded, alone, isolated from anyone who might care. Even in the presence of someone else, there's an inescapable loneliness. Though it may not appear to help, having someone to provide a different view of circumstances can lead to solutions. There are usually positive aspects of a situation that we miss on our own. The right friend can be like a valuable coach on the sidelines, helping us see what we might have missed.

The isolation of depression is counter to the freedom necessary to practice jiu jitsu effectively. It's not your own limbs that need to be manipulated, but those of the opponent. A hermit cannot practice jiu jitsu. You need a partner.

And that is so often what's missing in the depressed person's experience. A partner in healing must listen unconditionally, and perhaps no greater attention is placed on the other than in a combative situation. Because jiu jitsu requires near constant physical contact, an exceptionally close connection is built between training partners. There is an intimacy that lives within the world of twisted limbs and strangles. A camaraderie that can only be experienced with the other.

Deep depression creates the feeling that there is no other. No one for you to turn to. No one who understands or wants to have any contact with you. You feel useless and helpless at once.

In jiu jitsu class, you don't feel useless. Even if it's your day to play the nail, you're helping your partners get better. You're also learning from your mistakes and building the resilience to keep coming back, even after a beating.

I dragged myself to the academy many days, whining about the cold weather and my own masochistic nature. I hated training at least a third of the time. But I had to do it.

When you're depressed, it feels like you can't do anything that you're supposed to do. Everyday chores seem impossible. Sometimes even getting out of bed feels monumental.

Now, imagine feeling that way, but getting up at 6:30 am anyway to go grapple a bunch of thirsty animals looking to take you out, so they can literally earn stripes on their belts. This was my life for years.

But normally, once I'd start training, all my problems would be forgotten. My body would take over, and I'd let the resulting physical exhaustion take care of the lingering internal pain. At the end of the session, my mind felt fresh while I was lying in a pool of sweat.

Physical exercise can work miracles on depression. Training releases endorphins — neurotransmitters that alleviate pain, improve mood, enhance well-being, and lower stress. Working out elevates testosterone, which regulates bone and muscle mass and increases strength, and it also improves mood. Growth hormone levels similarly increase during exercise, promoting both physical well-being and mental acuity.

In the case of ADHD, a lack of dopamine kills motivation. The brain produces this hormone and neurotransmitter, which sends messages throughout the body and helps regulate mood and motivation. Someone deficient in dopamine has reward circuits that aren't operating correctly, and without being able to envision the benefit of an activity, action is difficult.

Dopamine deficiencies also lead to depression. People living with depression can feel both down about themselves and unmotivated to do anything about it.

I don't know where I'd be if I didn't feel a responsibility to be on the mat for class when I felt at my worst. Sometimes I'd even cry because I couldn't imagine facing the world, let alone putting on my gi and fighting. Without knowing my professor and teammates were counting on me to show up, I might have blown off the classes and never continued my martial arts journey. Depression might have swallowed me up.

Good jiu jitsu requires movement, and so does battling depression. You won't always feel your best, but you have to keep moving to find your opportunities. It only takes the right angle to help you escape a seemingly hopeless situation.

Chapter 16: Wanting to Quit

Key Takeaways

1 Depression feels like the moment you want to quit in a tough match.

2 Building your frame is essential.

3 Be firm, but pliable.

4 Overthinking will freeze you.

5 Jiu jitsu isn't practiced in isolation, and nothing makes you feel more isolated than depression.

6 When you grind through, you eventually find some space to escape.

SECTION 4: COMMITTING TO YOURSELF

"The Dip is the long, hard journey between beginner's luck and real accomplishment."

— Seth Godin, *The Dip*

CHAPTER 17
Hammers and Nails

Only dismantling your persona, the mask you wear for the public, leads to true progress. While there is concern over appearances, energy will be expended preserving what is, rather than creating something new.

Combat sports require you to strip away facades, or they will be ripped to shreds by your opponent. Reputation, belt color, education — none of that matters when you're working to sharpen your fighting skills. The mat is an equalizer that sifts away the mentally weak.

Only .06 percent of the US population are victims of violent crime every year, according to Statista Research Department. (Although violent crime, particularly domestic violence, goes under-reported because victims are often unable or unwilling to reach out to police due to fear or shame.) Yet it seems the media portrays 90 percent of what happens in the world as potentially catastrophic. It's a wonder many more people aren't learning to fight.

As much as you shouldn't wish for a fight, the street is the ultimate proving ground. If you avoid or survive just one violent altercation because of your training, a lifetime of membership dues have paid for themselves. I've had multiple students avoid fights simply by getting into their stances. Their assailants reconsidered once they saw there would be some resistance.

Gaining the proficiency to pull off a move under pressure on the street takes dedication and an admiration for the art form. Though they're doing what they love, the people on the mat suffer willingly. They expose their bodies to daily beatings that 98 percent of people won't so the techniques will flow naturally when they need them.

> A study published by the Statista Research Department suggests that 2 percent of US citizens, or about 6 million people, participate in martial arts.[7]

In order to learn to apply their craft realistically and effectively, they must endure many more moments of defeat than victory. And they must return day after day, willing to do it again, even when there seems to be no reward in sight.

These seekers will question themselves many times during their journeys. If you're in your right mind, you're bound to question your willingness to swap blood, sweat, and tears with compatriots who are hellbent on choking you unconscious, punching you in the liver, or kicking you in the head.

Some people think masochism is a mental disorder. Experiencing enjoyment from feeling pain is seen as twisted. There must be something wrong with you if you choose to feel pain. We should avoid pain at all costs.

But not everyone lives life this way. For a select few, pain plus purpose equals pleasure.

The eternal road to martial arts mastery is paved with pain. It's a road no one is dragged onto kicking and screaming (unless you're a little kid being forced to take taekwondo classes). You have to want to get good. It doesn't happen by accident. Yes, you can have talent, and that can help, but it will only get you so far.

Lots of the talented ones quit early. The realization hits that it's not all knockouts and submissions, and that the hammer must sometimes play the nail. It's too much for some egos to take. They fear the destruction of their invincible persona can't be survived. They're wrong.

Chapter 17: Hammers and Nails

"Success is no accident. It is hard work, perseverance, learning, studying, sacrifice and most of all, love of what you are doing or learning to do."

– Pele

Jobbers

Some guys spend most of their time as the nail. They don't get much hammer time. They're the "Brooklyn Brawlers" of martial arts.

The Brawler was the World Wrestling Federation wrestler who lost every TV match he was in. He was a jobber — his only purpose was to lose and sell the fight to the crowd. To make the other guy a star.

Real life jobbers are often trying to prove something to someone who hurt them in the past as well as to themselves. They need to know they can take any beating life has to offer, physical or otherwise, and not be broken. Those guys can be a danger to themselves. Sometimes, they don't know when to quit.

Some practitioners on the mat are there for other people to sharpen their techniques on. As long as both athletes are getting something out of the situation, and there isn't any bullying going on, you can learn a lot from just getting good at defense. Defense may even be more likely to protect you on the street than offense would.

Those metaphorical punching bags are the ones to be admired the most — the punching bag who comes in every day and knows he is going to lose. Everyone knows he's going to be the easiest matchup. But he comes in every day and takes his licks, knowing he'll get better for it. He does.

Jobbers are appreciated by their teams for their devout perseverance. They're usually the friendliest guys in the class, and generally lighten up the room. They are the most egoless in the bunch. No one is looking to mercilessly beat up on the jobbers.

A jobber won't have a target on their back — not to the leaders of the class. That's what makes jiu jitsu so special. The leaders will want to make that person feel good. They'll lift them up, while also being able to practice whatever they want. Both people will win in the match, because each will learn, not just the stronger of the two.

There are also professional nails who turn into certified hammers. It doesn't always start off as the goal, because some jobbers are such nice guys, but eventually, through years of practice, the transition just happens. They go from frightened nail to feared hammer before they even know it.

I have a friend who was so disliked as a white belt at a very well-known BJJ and MMA (mixed martial arts) gym that an up-and-coming MMA fighter invited him to spar — and beat him down viciously to try to get my friend to quit. This happened repeatedly at the hands of the same fighter, but twelve years later, my buddy earned his black belt and his teammates' respect.

> It's poor etiquette to turn down a higher belt who wants to spar.

The growth my friend experienced during his journey far surpassed the reward of that piece of red tipped, dyed black cloth. He proved to himself that he could overcome human resistance, multiple surgeries, divorce, and terrible trauma to achieve a long-term goal that ultimately only mattered to him. That's hard to put a price on.

Chapter 17: Hammers and Nails

Key Takeaways

1	Trying to preserve your persona will impede your growth.
2	There is a certain masochism to combat sports training.
3	Some days, you will be the hammer. Other days, you will be the nail. Enjoy both.
4	With practice, full-time nails can become certified hammers.

CHAPTER 18
Playing Hurt

Pop! The pain was excruciating. For the better part of my martial arts career, one of my knees would dislocate in training. Most of the time it would be from positions that didn't put me in an awkward contortion. I just had so little stability from damage to my meniscus and ACL that my knee would slide out of place every now and then. I'd scream every time from the pain.

The hammer does not escape unscathed.

When you're a young athlete, you feel invincible. You never envision your body breaking down. The first time you sustain a major injury, the illusion of indestructibility is shattered. You suddenly feel your mortality for the first time.

If an injury becomes chronic, then you feel like damaged goods. It's as if you've been cheated by the athletic gods — given a passion to practice but not an adequate vehicle. There's a lot of asking, "Why me?"

> A physical injury that keeps you away from your sport can hurt as much as the emotional pain of losing someone or something you love. Sometimes, you'd rather deal with the pain than give up what you care about.

I kept training through the injuries because I felt I had to. Quitting wasn't an option. Martial arts had become my life, and playing hurt was how I showed my dedication.

When my knee would pop out, my leg would be stuck in a slightly bent position. My professor would come up and grab my ankle as I lay on my back. He'd ask me to relax, and he'd yank my leg so the knee popped back in place, like you see people do with dislocated shoulders. Once that glorious click signaled relief, I'd get right back to training.

Sometimes, the pull wouldn't work, and he'd just be yanking on my leg until I couldn't take the pain anymore. The leg could stay that way for days, slightly bent and swollen, before randomly popping back on its own.

The first time I tore my knee was in judo class. It was around 2002, and I was in my mid-twenties. A larger classmate fell on my leg awkwardly, and I was out of training for nine months. I was heartbroken because I was fairly close to getting my judo black belt when it happened, and a huge part of my identity was suddenly taken away. But I shifted my attention, and used that time to write and produce a play that my classmates and instructors came out to watch. When my sensei saw I'd written some judo moves into the script, he told me it looked like I was ready to come back to training. I did soon after.

> When your identity is challenged by your life circumstances, have something constructive you can shift your attention to.

Each time I got hurt and had to take time off, I felt as if my life was incomplete. I wasn't letting out a certain kind of energy I needed to release at that time in my life. Luckily, writing filled the void when I couldn't train, and performing on stage got out some of that physical energy. But for some people, being out injured leaves them sad and out of shape.

Even when I was injured in jiu jitsu, I'd come in to watch classes. You can learn a lot from watching other people train, and there are always new details to pick up. Jiu Jitsu is so addictive, and the atmosphere is so welcoming, that there's a point in your journey when you'd rather be at the academy than anywhere else in the world, even if you're just there as a spectator.

The Initiation

My brown belt test is legendary. At the time, I was only the second person to test for that rank at our academy. Because I also managed and taught at the school, my test had to set an example.

> Most BJJ schools don't test for belts. The instructor simply hands you the belt when he believes you're ready. My instructor, though Brazilian, liked the idea of demonstrating technical knowledge along with physical ability under the pressure of an exam format, especially for non-competitors. Competitors are often promoted on the podium.

All the adult students from the school lined up along the side of the wall, out the door, and down the hall. I had to take on each one of them — first with a gi, then without a gi, and finally in a mixed martial arts round with striking.

No-gi jiu jitsu is much faster paced because there's no gripping the kimono to slow things down. Competitors quickly get slippery and are more difficult to control. The matches are grueling, and the more explosive practitioner often has the advantage. By the time I got to the no-gi round, I was already exhausted.

A little more than halfway through the test, my left pectoral muscle tore. I finished out the round and took a break. My professor asked me if I needed to quit, and I said no. I'll never forget his words.

"That's what I want to hear."

So, the beating continued. A professional MMA fighter who happened to be in town came in and saw what was happening. He said it looked like a gang initiation.

I finished the rest of the test by only using my right arm. It was mostly me trying to survive the entire time, but I did, and it was one of my proudest moments in martial arts. At the time, I felt inadequate for not wiping the floor with the whole school at once, but in retrospect, I performed the best I could and showed heart.

To the outside observer, there may have been no benefit to going through such an ordeal. My ex-wife thought the beating I took that day might have changed my brain, and that I started acting differently afterward. I can't deny that I've thought about it myself. Still, I learned I can deal with more adversity than I thought I could, and I developed a new level of resilience because of the challenge.

The academy never had a test like that again.

In Sickness and in Health

In 2017, while training for the World Masters Championships, I dislocated my left ring finger when my opponent broke my grip off his collar. The digit was facing completely to the left. There was no popping this back in.

I had to go into surgery to get the finger fixed. That meant cutting my wedding ring off. My marriage was rocky at the time, and it all seemed pretty symbolic.

I'd already registered and bought airline tickets for the championship tournament in Las Vegas, so I wasn't going to let the finger stop me. I wore a cast for the last three weeks of training and only used my right hand. The cast came off the day before our flight to Vegas. Still, I had a good showing at the tournament. Although I lost my third match, I was incredibly proud of myself for finding a way to compete. But boy was that finger killing me afterward.

I don't regret any of the times I played hurt, although I'm sure I caused additional damage because I wouldn't just rest. Each time I was injured, I would question the severity of my pain, and whether I was just punking out by not stepping on the mat. I had to prove to myself that I wasn't making excuses.

Discomfort isn't something everyone trains themselves for. To a lot of people, discomfort is a sign to quit. People surrender to pain too quickly. I never wanted to be one of those people.

Chapter 18: Playing Hurt

To me, discomfort signifies the time to choose whether you will accept a challenge or back away. Anyone can keep going when it's easy and fun. But can you persevere when you're battered and bruised?

I imagine some part of me must have wanted to be injured. I either needed to rest, or slow down, or listen to something my body was telling me. Maybe I needed to make time for something I was neglecting, and the only way to get my attention was with an injury.

Sometimes we play hurt because we're stubborn, and we really should be resting. But other times, it's important to ask ourselves if we can play through the pain. Will it injure us worse if we stick it out? Can we push just a little more?

Through years of experience, and getting to know your body and its tendencies, it becomes easier to discern between serious injuries and inconveniences. A chronic injury should be tended to before returning to the mat if you ever want to get better. A muscle, tendon, or ligament that's partially torn is going to get worse with more training. An injured digit or sore elbow can probably be played through.

The little cumulative injuries, especially pain in the fingers (from gripping), knee, or back pain will make training a drag sometimes. Those are the days you have to push through, and maybe train lighter while still getting some movement going and practicing technique.

Some injuries heal themselves. Others just need a little tug, and they'll pop right back in. Some might even require going under the knife. Boo boos happen, it's whether you let them hurt you beyond the surface that matters. Will your identity be shattered, or have you built the kind of foundation that can withstand cracks in your facade?

Key Takeaways

1 Injuries are part of jiu jitsu just like pain is part of life.

2 Your emotional response to that pain or injury dictates whether you see it as something you can conquer or not.

3 Some pain is a message for you to slow down.

4 You have to weigh the pros and cons of playing hurt.

CHAPTER 19
Getting over the Hump

In Seth Godin's book *The Dip*, he describes the titular period of time after your initial excitement for a project when you hit a plateau or simply don't enjoy the activity anymore. You're not having fun.

I used to think that was the time to quit. Life is supposed to be fun, so why should I grind through something I'm not enjoying? On to the next thing.

But when something starts out as fun and stops being fun because it suddenly got hard, that's likely a sign that you need to keep going. On the other side of the grind is fun and knowledge together — the ability to flow.

The only way to take your mind out of an activity is to have it ingrained in your body. Getting something right usually means getting it wrong first. Enough wrong attempts, and you get discouraged. Stopping now is a mistake.

That discouragement needs to turn into determination. Like a bully that keeps pushing you back into the sand, learning a difficult skill will make you fall over and over again. Getting up takes a willingness to risk defeat.

If you don't believe there's mastery on the other side of the wall you keep smashing into, then you won't keep trying to break through. The more difficult a goal, the more you can be certain that completing the task will bring great reward. It may not be the reward you expected, but the resilience built while pursuing a goal transforms a person.

Still, you must be ready to change course when it becomes apparent you're getting nowhere. A goal that remains out of reach despite you seeing it on the horizon for an eternity may take a different approach than the one you've become accustomed to. Retreat, regroup, and attack again. And there will even be times you'll determine it's just not worth it to go on. The goal doesn't matter anymore. That's when you're ready to move on.

I wanted to quit many times while pursuing my black belts. Training became a nuisance that came along with bumps and bruises. I'd have to literally roll myself out of bed and onto the floor before standing up because I was in so much pain all the time. I also felt tremendous pressure to perform in training because I was an instructor. I left myself no room to fail on the mat, and all the fun was sucked out of the activity.

> Keeping yourself physically fit for training is essential. Some extra resistance exercise will give you a protective outer shell and strengthen muscle and connective tissue. While nothing can mimic jiu jitsu with a partner, a physique with a little extra body armor will help you stay healthy. A good amount of sleep and a balanced diet will keep your engine running smoothly.

If my entire life wasn't wrapped up in martial arts, maybe I would've quit. But I had my school and all my students, and I was close to getting my third black belt. I had invested too much.

That's what you have to do with some things. You need to invest so much that you can't go back. You're closer to the finish than you are to the start. The road to black belt feels long while you're on it. It's a blast sometimes, at others it's a backbreaking trek that you have no idea why you're on. At blue belt, you're soaking it all up. At purple, you think you're hot shit. At brown, you want the next level.

It's hard not to think ahead — to want to get there now. The things we envision for ourselves take an interval before they become part of our reality. Becoming frustrated by the length of that interval will get you to quit.

A goal can be divided into three sections: The moment of conception; the work; and the reward. In many cases, the reward is only the achievement of the goal. The personal sense of accomplishment may be the only prize from your long and difficult journey.

That has to be enough. If it's not, and you know it at inception, don't even bother.

Key Takeaways

1	The time to quit isn't when things get tough.
2	Nothing will hold that initial excitement forever. You have to do the work for the work's sake.
3	Discouragement must turn into determination.
4	Understand that once you've had your brilliant idea, you'll need to put in the work to manifest it.
5	Don't be thrown off by the interval from conception to manifestation.
6	If doing the work isn't enough reward, don't even start.

CHAPTER 20
The Black Belt

There is a scourge in the martial arts world. It's driven by greed. It's been around for decades, with as much of a chance of being eliminated as capitalism itself.

McDojos are martial arts schools that operate as belt factories. The schools charge students for promotions who aren't ready for the next rank. Belt factories in other styles promote children to black belt, a rank that should indicate the ability to defend oneself effectively as well as a deep knowledge of the art gained through years of experience. But it's not just kids getting the belt that aren't ready. Adults can buy their way to belts, through money or favors. Of course, this builds a false sense of security, because one buys into their own hype as a "black belt." As a result, these places have watered down the black belt to the point that the belt color means little when it comes to skill.

A blue belt from a great academy will be better than a black belt from a McDojo. This can lead to exposing the illegitimate black belt when training with people from other schools. I remember always feeling a little awkward when I was a lower belt sparring with a black belt from another school who I was beating. It felt disrespectful to me, so I would always dial it back, so they could save face.

No one is going to dial it back for you in the street, but it's not these students' fault that their skill isn't quite where it should be. It's the fault of the system they're a part of.

McDojos do a disservice to society. They siphon the money of unsuspecting, uninformed, and eventually delusional people who don't know what real fighting feels like. Parents often don't even know what style their kids are studying. They just call everything "karate."

The Value of the Black Belt

A black belt only means something for one reason. The struggle to get there is all that matters, and if you didn't struggle all that much, it's just a piece of cloth. Sure, struggle means different things to different people, but a black belt shouldn't be like a "FINISHER" T-shirt from a endurance race. No offense to finishers.

I was offered a taekwondo black belt for $300 by an unscrupulous school owner before I opened my academy, despite never having taken an official taekwondo class in my life. Admittedly, I thought about the extra diploma hanging on my wall before politely turning him down.

A black belt should be an elite symbol for making it through an extended, grueling, ego-shattering period of training that made you a better fighter and person. It's not something everyone has the fortitude to accomplish.

Black belts should be able to practically use their skills to defend themselves. If this isn't the case, then they've been cheated. The "martial" in martial arts literally means warlike. Yes, we might take it metaphorically at times, but if that's what you're after, play chess.

Martial arts are special because they allow us to cultivate our physical and intellectual sides en route to achieving mastery over ourselves and our opponents in the most primal way possible. There is no sport older than fighting. Knowing how to physically defeat a larger opponent builds the confidence to never feel the need to dominate another person. The self-esteem forged by training can turn a timid child into a fierce warrior and help them cunningly slay the evil giant in their path.

To feel the full effects of martial arts, and for the black belt to be worth far more than its weight, the practitioner must have been pressure tested. They must have been faced with opponents fighting at or near full capacity, and with full contact. If they have only practiced their techniques against air or achieved their black belt with limited contact with other humans, then the belt is worthless.

Chapter 20: The Black Belt

How Did This Happen?

Despite how much I dreamed of achieving my Brazilian jiu jitsu black belt, once I got it, I didn't think I deserved it. I felt I wasn't ready.

This seems to be the common reaction to receiving the belt. I remember getting a call from a friend of mine after he got promoted to black belt. He had never had more self-doubt. How could he live up to the rank? His instructor must have made a mistake.

I assured him that if our professor decided he was ready, then he was. And I told him my own story. I felt unworthy after my promotion. Although I had put my time in and already achieved black belts in Japanese jiu jitsu and judo, I still felt unworthy of the BJJ belt.

Brazilian jiu jitsu had such a mystical quality to it that the belt seemed like the holy grail to me before I had one. It's the same for everyone. Once you get there, you can't imagine you're now like one of those people you admired when you were a lower belt. You're at the front of the line now. Suddenly, you're posing in black belt only photos and being treated with more respect by fellow students. The belt comes with an aura you're not sure you're worthy of emanating.

It wasn't until I started getting pulled into those photos that I began to feel like a part of the club. Being accepted, acknowledged, and appreciated by my coaches and peers made the difference for me.

The things we fight hard to get, and even daydream about, may feel too big for us once we're up close — face to face with what we imagined. Dreams are seen as unachievable for a lot of people who won't even try.

But if you're willing to give it a shot, you should know everyone feels like an impostor once they get to where they want to go. If you don't go through at least a little bit of that, you might have a huge ego. Or you might just be the most secure person in the world.

Key Takeaways

1	If a goal becomes a commodity, someone will be willing to sell it to you.
2	The value of the goal diminishes if you didn't really work for it.
3	Being authentic requires feeling secure in your abilities.
4	If your abilities haven't been pressure tested, you can't have full faith in them.
5	We all get impostor syndrome sometimes (some of us feel it more than others).

CHAPTER 21
The Arm Collectors

The guard position in jiu jitsu is when a player is lying on their back or sitting on the ground. To keep a player in your guard you need to keep them from passing your legs. As long as your opponent doesn't get past your legs, you've retained your guard.

Sometimes, you'll have your opponent between both legs (full guard) or just one leg (half guard). Other times you'll be sitting and using your hands and feet to gain control. Either way, the guard is not a disadvantageous position if you know how to use it.

I used to train with an Israeli soldier who was a demon from his back. Any time you were stuck inside his full guard, you were in grave danger. He was able to lift his hips off the ground so quickly that if you left your elbow past his belly button for a fraction of a second, he would put you in an arm lock, attacking your elbow when the limb went straight, and applying pressure that could break the joint. He was what you could call an arm collector.

Arm collectors are scary. A choke just puts you to sleep. An arm lock that is put on too fast for you to tap will leave you with elbow pain for months. Years of getting arm locked (and kicked in the arm during striking training) left me with tendinitis and bone fragments floating around my elbow.

Joint locks are designed to maim. The tearing of tendons and ligaments and breaking of bones isn't gentle. While getting to the position is artistic, the result is brutal. Just knowing the potential of a strong arm bar is enough to strike fear. The arm collector goes into the fight with the advantage of having his partner on edge because the end can happen so quickly.

Yet in training, we can use these techniques without hurting our opponent, as long as they submit when they feel the pressure. As frightening as the prospect of getting caught in a tight arm bar is, you're not afraid of getting hurt. You just don't want to tap.

Still, there's something that feels more violent about arm locks. Those specializing in them are like hunters, waiting for the limb to be left out in the open so they can pounce. A good arm collector will get it from nearly every position, transitioning from body control or choke to an arm attack seamlessly.

Arm collectors don't hesitate when they see what they want. An arm that isn't attacked immediately when it's left out on its lonesome will soon move out of range.

The limb has to be controlled by the attacker's entire body, so there's no chance for the single arm to fight back. Fully committing all of oneself to the singular cause is the only way to get the submission.

But attacking before control is established will allow an opponent to easily escape, so although you can't hesitate, you can't rush either.

> In modern day jiu jitsu, the heel hook is the most feared submission. The leg lock twists the knee and happens so quickly that tapping in time is sometimes impossible. The move must be performed slower than normal in training.

Attacking Like an Arm Collector

Anyone who is goal-oriented has an arm collector's attitude. They see something they want, and they commit to getting it. They strike when the opportunity is there and don't try to make things happen before their time. And once it's there for the taking, they take that arm home with them as a trophy.

Lots of people never even try to attack the arm off their backs. The move requires one to uncross their ankles when they have their legs wrapped around their partner's waist. This is referred to as closed guard and is the safest position to be in when you're on your back. Attacking the arm means opening the guard to throw your hips up, leaving a path for your partner to escape.

You have to be confident to be an arm collector. Patient yet self-assured. You have to believe you'll be able to get that arm when you go for it, or you won't even try. Or if you do try, you'll fail from lack of commitment. You won't throw your hips up high enough. You won't hold the arm secure enough. You'll blow the submission because you don't believe.

That was my professor's favorite coaching instruction. When you were going for a move, he would simply yell, "Believe!" It worked a lot of the time.

It wasn't that the words were magical, but sometimes when you're close to pulling something off, you can't believe it's actually working. Coach's words were positive reinforcement. We all need that.

Taking an arm collector's approach to life can get you a long way. Secure your target. Commit all you have. Be patient. Take risks. Believe in your position. Apply just the right amount of pressure, bending your opponent without breaking them. Don't stop until the opposition surrenders.

Key Takeaways

1 An arm collector is very dangerous off his back, a position most people think is disadvantageous.

2 An arm collector's attitude takes patience, full commitment, and no hesitation.

3 Better to submit before you break — and fight another day — in one piece.

SECTION 5: CHOOSING YOUR COMMUNITY

"We yearn for an unquestioned experience of belonging, to feel at home with ourselves and others, at ease and fully accepted. But the trance of unworthiness keeps the sweetness of belonging out of reach."

— Tara Brach, *Radical Acceptance*

CHAPTER 22
Choosing the Right Academy

Some academies are all about competition. The competitors get the majority of the attention, and training is always hardcore. There isn't much room for soccer moms or Zen pacifists at these places. They only know one training speed — all out.

Other academies are all about being chill. Fun is emphasized in training, and anyone from any walk of life can come in and have a good workout. These types of schools are great for socializing and building camaraderie.

My own academy, Omni Martial Arts, was a great balance of family atmosphere and competition. Our competitors were successful, but we also had accountants, carpenters, cops, doctors, and housewives all sweating and learning together. We would socialize, throw parties, and all show up to support our competition team.

My students' Facebook group was called Omni Fam. Several of my students met and had children while training at my school. It became so common that I got ordained so I could perform my students' wedding ceremonies.

> The most important thing in choosing an academy, above a fancy website or a list of championship accomplishments, is the vibe of the school. Without visiting the academy and getting a sense of the atmosphere, it's impossible to know if it's a good fit for you.

Just as the adults in your life always said to choose your friends wisely, pick your academy cautiously. Some academies are bastions of gossip. Most often, avoiding this means staying out of cliques. Adults are no different than high school kids in that respect. They will gravitate to like-minded individuals, and in an academy, it only takes one bad seed to spread a corrosive atmosphere.

Often these corrosive elements will ingrain themselves in the culture of the school to the point that the fate of the academy hinges on the culprit not causing a disruption.

The Perfect Cult

Academy culture is usually a reflection of its head professor. Academies that bestow a grandiose aura around their leader create opportunities for the misuse of power. Some of these schools take on cult-like atmospheres, the professors instilling fear in their disciples.

Martial arts schools are kind of the perfect place to build a cult. The leader stands at the front of the room every day, and has his adoring students bow to him. He wears a distinct color belt or uniform that separates him from the rest. He has an important sounding title, like sensei, sifu, guru, or master. He bestows honors on you by promoting you. His praise lifts you up, and his disappointment crushes your heart. You want nothing more than to please your dear leader.

Followers fall into a cult leader's grasp because they believe they've found something they were missing. They believe the leader is the embodiment of who they should be. A nefarious front man might twist this adoration into something dark. He might use it to control the actions and thoughts of his followers. Once he has their trust, they'll believe any lie he feeds them.

Over the past several years, there have been multiple scandals associated with well-known jiu jitsu academies. Accusations of sexual misconduct have run rampant, exposing some organizations' cultures of misogyny and abuse.

Chapter 22: Choosing the Right Academy

One such case involved a very well-known jiu jitsu guru whose academy was among the top American competition schools. This professor is large and imposing, and he used his size and presence to instill both fear and respect in his team. He demanded absolute loyalty and allegedly sexually assaulted female students. Members of his team were accused of rape, and he was once charged in a gang assault of a woman. Most of his top students left his fighter housing under cover of night because of their fear. These were all top-level trained martial artists. They were terrified of the persona their professor had created.

Another high-level team has been accused of shielding a pedophile who taught at the school. The head professor, a legendary competitor, allegedly pleaded for the loyal young victim to be silent.

I've known a few creepers from the martial arts scene. Most who you wouldn't expect. All of them used their power as higher belts to manipulate and take advantage of victims who were in a physically compromising position. The trust that was damaged could be irreconcilable.

Toxic cultures like the ones described above can only be created under the guidance of someone who will look the other way or facilitate the drama themselves. But there are less pervasive ways a school can corrode from the inside. And there are some tell tale signs of good and bad places to train.

The academy head that won't allow himself to be seen as flawed is protecting a fragile ego. That in itself is a barrier to him being the best instructor he can be. He holds himself back by not being genuine, and this will come across in his teaching.

At my fortieth birthday party, all my students went around in a circle and spoke about what I meant to them. When the microphone finally got to my best friend, he proclaimed, "I had no idea Julio would have his own cult one day."

It was kinda starting to feel that way.

But our cult wasn't up to any bad stuff. I wasn't trying to convince anyone we were going to get beamed up into the mother ship or getting them to drink the Kool-Aid. I was professing clean living, hard training, and having fun. My school was known as the party school. Our Christmas soirees were legendary.

While my academy was at its peak, I'm convinced we had the perfect balance of kindness and legit badassery. I'm proud of what we built at that place, and you should be proud of the academy you're a part of. Remember, the company you keep matters. They can lift you up or smother you into the mat.

Key Takeaways

1	Choosing an academy is like choosing a home. You have to feel comfortable.
2	Some academies devolve into cults, with the instructor as their leader.
3	Steer clear of cliques. Be an individual.
4	Like with everything, seek a balance of hard and soft.
5	Remember, training should be fun.
6	Join a school that has heart in all respects.

CHAPTER 23
Picking the Right Partners

When the bell rings after a round of rolling, and there's a mad scramble to switch partners, sometimes you just grab whoever is closest to you. You might luck out and have a graceful gazelle to spar with, or you might end up with a bull looking for a china shop.

Those bulls are a pain in the ass to control. You've got to grab hold of them tightly, or they'll trample all over you. It's not a lot of fun sparring a bull, unless you're a matador. If you can get out of the way each time they try to smash you, you can have a little fun with it. But if you're in their path and leave them free to control you, you're in for a bad day.

The gazelles are fun to flow with. They glide from move to move, and occasionally show some flash. They aren't trying to take your arm or neck home with them. When you get them, they tap and say good job. When they get you, you do the same. You've both learned a new move after the match. You don't have to worry about a knee to the face or an elbow to the groin. Gazelles are the best.

The Perfect Session

The perfect training session would have you train with someone at your level, someone better than you, and someone lower level than you. The highest-level person gives you the challenge you need to get you to the next step and helps you practice your defense. The equal helps you expose your own flaws and strengths. The inferior competitor is there for you to practice new techniques and combinations, but also to become a better teacher yourself.

Partners shouldn't be picked at random. They should have a purpose. Generally speaking, when I teach jiu jitsu, I like to pair up the students myself. In the event that the pairs choose, I adjust accordingly, switching people around as I see fit. Not all body or personality types work well together. It could be counterproductive to have the wrong duo trying to learn from each other.

For many of us, we've approached our relationships like we're scrambling in between rounds, attaching ourselves to whoever is closest out of convenience. We haven't given any thought to whether or not this is someone we can learn from, and someone who can learn from us.

Patience is what's missing. Fear of being alone makes many of us jump the gun on relationships. Friendships are forced upon us by the walls of a workplace or school. The time and freedom to choose our own acquaintances might find us with a whole new entourage.

Overlooking obvious flaws becomes unnecessary when you're not in a rush to find companionship. If you're not willing to say no to a relationship when red flags pop up, what does it say about your state of mind? Is your self-esteem so low you'd rather settle than face solitude?

Sometimes the red flags we ignore are flaws that subconsciously attract us to that person. Those flaws may remind us of someone from our past, and we may have unknowingly convinced ourselves that we deserve more of the same. So, we miraculously keep ending up with precisely who we don't want.

I would commonly overlook flaws in friends because I thought the outcast should always be befriended. What I didn't realize is that sometimes people are outcasts because they're assholes.

> **You can't befriend everyone, nor should you want to.**

Some training partners may be brutes, but those people give you a chance to practice controlling a brute. That's a good skill to have. As the class enforcer at one point, I was expected to go with any brute who walked through the door. It wasn't always fun, but the experience prepared me for sparring sessions that can feel nightmarish to other people. I had regular sparring partners who were extremely heavy and hard to move, and I had other partners who moved so much they were nearly impossible to catch. I had partners who were guard players — who fought off their backs — and other partners who preferred to fight from top position. I had flexible partners and strong but stiff partners. Each style has its own strengths and weaknesses, and I learned from each one.

It's important to have friends and acquaintances who you elevate, who elevate you, and some with whom you have a common perspective. This doesn't always come from one individual. Often, the people in our lives serve a specific purpose. They may be our black belt sparring partners who always give us the tough but wise advice that might hurt at first, but that makes us better in the end. They may be the eager blue belts trying to prove they're ready to be teachers by sharing their meager experience, when they know just as little as us. Or they may be the doe-eyed white belt who looks to us for guidance and can't imagine us being flawed.

> You should choose three types of partners (on and off the mat): those who you elevate, those who elevate you, and those with whom you are comparable.

They all serve a purpose to us, just like we serve a purpose to them. It may not always seem balanced, but somehow, it is. Through a grapevine of connections that are too entangled for us to figure out, everyone is fulfilling everyone else's needs.

The Power of Teaching

In teaching, we're forced not only to repeat movements again and again, but also to break them down into their smallest components. Jiu jitsu teachers should include as much detail as they can, so the technique is demonstrated verbally and visually. In this way, every type of learner will benefit from the lesson.

Meanwhile, the instructor has heard herself explain out loud what has only been in her head until now. She has breathed new life into the technique for herself by thinking of it in new ways.

It's rare that we take such opportunities in our everyday lives. Being mindful enough to break down our every movement would take more hours than there are in a day. But in breaking down a move, what appears to be one fluid motion can have a dozen moving parts — if deconstructed enough. Performing the wrong step in the sequence can wreck your plans.

The learning process shouldn't only be left to the teacher at the head of the class. Each student should take their education into their own hands by dissecting their own technique and teaching themselves how to make their jiu jitsu better. As each practitioner progresses, they'll teach lower belts in order to gain practice and improve their own game.

Knowledge should be shared, not only because it enriches others, but also because teaching reinforces one's own connection to the information. We can sharpen our skills by spreading what we know, while helping our fellow practitioner get ahead. Everybody wins.

Key Takeaways

1 If we settle for low hanging fruit, we limit our choices and experiences.

2 You should choose three types of partners (on and off the mat): those who you elevate, those who elevate you, and those with whom you are comparable.

3 Each level of partner, like each person in your life, serves a specific purpose for you, just as you do for them.

4 If you want to learn more, teach.

CHAPTER 24
Loyalty

Jiu jitsu schools have been territorial in the past. Although it's gotten better, with more athletes training at different academies, tribalism still exists. At tournaments, schools hang their flags from the rafters and chant in unison. They throw up gang-like hand gestures representing their academies. There's never a question what school everyone is from.

This competition attitude extends to the training room. It's highly discouraged by many coaches for students to train at other academies. Academy patches are mandatory on uniforms. Some old school coaches get downright offended if you train elsewhere. It's as if their special knowledge isn't to be shared with anyone else.

Modern practitioners enjoy pilgrimages to new academies. The opportunity to meet people and roll with different bodies is cherished. There are seminars and camps around the world that attract international attendees. Some of the more popular, prize-winning academies are landmarks in their own right, with daily visitors from across the globe.

This is a far cry from the old days, and a refreshing change. Practitioners can now exchange techniques they've never been exposed to before. Real-life friendships are built through the interchange of students from school to school. A true BJJ community emerges, not separated by academy logos or slogans, but only under the banner of the gentle art itself.

The Ronin

A ronin is a samurai without a master. He is banished to roam alone, with no real home. Those of us who have cut ties with our academies and have yet to find a home refer to ourselves as ronin.

The academy becomes a second home to most of us, with some people spending more time with their teammates than with their own families. Teams travel together, compete together, party together, sweat together (and on each other), and generally get as physically close as two humans can platonically get.

The bond that's built is indescribable when you have each other's lives in your hands during training. If someone holds on to a choke for too long, they could literally kill their partner. A submission applied irresponsibly can leave someone maimed.

The old Japanese jiu jitsu fighters would practice their techniques on civilians to ensure they would work on the street. There was no camaraderie, only combat. Modern grappling, and BJJ in particular, have turned a combative experience into a social exercise. The combining of the two is a great representation of the yin and yang that encompasses jiu jitsu.

When the bond between a practitioner and his academy is broken, he loses more than a coach. More than training partners. More than friends or mentors. He loses a secondary family, with whom he has shared his failures and victories. He loses people who have cheered him on at every step along the way — despite trying to kill him every day. In some cases, he loses the only social outlet he has.

Those are all good excuses to remain loyal. Fear of change will always try to keep you frozen, but it's no reason to stay in a bad spot. You'll make friends somewhere else. You'll find a new coach. You don't owe loyalty to a bad situation.

> If things no longer feel right where you are, it's time to move on.

Loyalty to Your Partner

The person you do owe loyalty to is the training partner you're working with in the moment. Their safety is your number one priority — even more than victory. There are certain maneuvers, such as spiking the head or bending the spine backwards, that can cause serious injury and can be done accidentally by inexperienced practitioners.

But no matter how careful you are, mishaps occur. Injuries happen. Part of loyalty and trust with your partner is to accept when an accident happens and move on. You don't hold a grudge, and you don't overreact and make a spectacle of yourself and your partner. You tape it up and you get back on the mat, or you sit on the side and observe.

In the event that your partner gets out of hand by playing wildly and irresponsibly, it's within your right to set him straight by applying some extra pressure or turning up your intensity. This is part of the loyalty pledge. I'll go as hard as you go.

From the moment you shake hands, bump fists, or bow before a match, you're making an unwritten agreement to treat each other with respect as combatants and martial artists. Nothing needs to be said.

This same respect should be afforded to everyone we come across, without judgment or preconceived notions of who they are or how they can benefit us in the exchange. One shouldn't need to demand courtesy or fair play; it should be understood without saying a word.

Loyalty to Yourself

Training can't be everything. In order to be a well-rounded human being, we need a variety of interests (or at least more than one). There are athletes who train all day long and play video games the rest of the time.

That actually sounds like an awesome existence for someone just starting out their adult life, but as you get older, there are other things that need your attention. Unless you are a professional competitor, training at the expense of family, friendships, or career can become detrimental.

Seek balance. Compartmentalize your training, so you can fully dedicate your attention to other things when necessary, and be most loyal to your own well-being.

Key Takeaways

1 Loyalty can become detrimental.

2 Broadening your horizons leads to making new, significant connections.

3 Your loyalty on the mat belongs to your training partner. Their safety is your top priority.

4 Unless you're a professional competitor, don't take training so seriously. Keep balance between training, family, work, and personal growth.

5 If things no longer feel right where you are, it's time to move on.

WRAP UP & RESOURCES

Post Training

I once did a speed networking event that lasted three minutes per person. In those three minutes, I had half the attendees telling me about their anxiety or fear.

Something happens to the people around you when you're open about your own problems. You'll get three types of reactions: They'll turn and run because they are afraid of their own feelings; they'll stay and listen because they feel a sense of obligation or genuine concern; or they'll lower their defenses and share their own stories with you.

A lot of my training partners came to me for advice about things because I never really hid what I was feeling, at least not at the end of class. By then, all the demons would've been exorcised, and I'd feel born again. I was open to sharing my deeper self, because my shell had been smashed apart in training.

So, when my classmates or students needed someone to talk to about their innermost thoughts and concerns, they'd often come to me. I felt as if it was a role I'd been born for because it seemed to come so naturally. I didn't seek to give advice, but I'd find just the right thing to say when someone needed to hear it.

What I learned most from those mat therapy sessions was that everyone is afraid of something. Often it's the people you think are most secure who carry the most fear. Hiding that fear is exhausting.

I suppose that's why I stopped hiding it. I was so ashamed of my feelings as a kid, particularly my anxiety, that I thought there was something wrong with me until I was in my late thirties. I thought no one else felt the kind of fear I did. I had to hide that I was afraid.

Now, I've embraced the fact that I feel heightened emotions compared to other people. While it often causes me distress, it also allows me to feel very high highs that other people don't experience.

Embracing that side of myself allows me to listen to people without judgment. I'm sure this is what draws people to me most, and why they feel willing to expose their own truths to me.

Martial arts gave me a platform to help people. From after training therapy to having my own academy, I found myself with an audience to share my experiences with. Writing has expanded this audience, but it still feels like those after training therapy sessions. I'm getting just as much out of it as my training partners are, and it feels like I'm in the right place.

I never imagined ten years ago that this would've been what I wanted; to write about martial arts and mental health. But the pieces in our lives decide how they'll come together. It may feel like you just keep picking up random parts along the way, but you're putting together a puzzle. You're gathering the pieces slowly, over a lifetime, so you might miss patterns if you're not paying attention.

It's our job to pay attention to connections so we see things we'll miss if we're sleepwalking. Seeing the whole picture from your vantage point is impossible. Often, the seemingly disparate parts of our lives fit in a way we don't expect. We can't force them to fit any other way.

All we can do is gather as many experiences as we can, learn from each one, and know it'll all make sense in the end.

Key Takeaways

1	Vulnerability lowers people's defenses.
2	While your experiences may feel scattered, they're part of a bigger picture.
3	Without conscious awareness, you will miss important connections.
4	We don't always get what we expect, but if we step back, it will make sense.

Resources

Recommended Reading

Brach, Tara. *Radical Acceptance*. 2003.
Godin, Seth. *The Dip*. 2007.
Musashi, Miyamoto. *The Book of Five Rings*. 1645.
Pressfield, Steven. *The War of Art*. 2002.
Van der Kolk, Bessel. *The Body Keeps the Score*. 2012.

Bibliography

1. Andrew Griffiths. The History of Fighting. Last modified 2025. https://www.historyoffighting.com/.
2. International Judo Federation. Last modified 2025. https://www.ijf.org.
3. James, Joshua. *2 Very Dangerous People Sharing 1 Small Space: A Play*. CreateSpace Independent Publishing Platform, 2015.
4. Ovid. *Metamorphoses*. Translated by Rolfe Humphries. Indiana University Press, 1955.
5. Blake, William. *The Marriage of Heaven and Hell*. Compiled by Geoffrey Keynes. Oxford University Press, 1975.
6. Watts, Alan. *The Way of Zen*. Vintage, 1999.
7. Statista Research Department. "Number of martial arts participants in the United States from 2010 to 2023." Statista. Last modified December 10, 2024. https://www.statista.com/statistics/191917/participants-in-martial-arts-in-the-us-since-2006/.

Acknowledgments

Special thanks to the great instructors who have helped me along my martial arts journey: Sensei Jack Krystek; Professor Vitor "Shaolin" Ribeiro; Coach Dave Siev; Coach Rick Bellot; and Coach Aziz Nabih. Each of these experts taught me a different facet of martial arts and expanded my knowledge so I could share what I learned with my students. I am forever grateful for their generosity.

I'd also like to acknowledge all the great mental health professionals I've worked with over the years, who have helped me navigate my internal world. Without these invaluable allies, my mind may have broken before my body gave way.

About the Author

JULIO ANGEL RIVERA is a writer, mental health advocate, and self-defense coach from NYC. Decades of training have shaped his philosophy, but just as important has been Julio's experience with trauma recovery, mindset and emotional regulation.

His first book, *Brokedown Sensei*, is available on Amazon. Julio's blog on the human condition can be found on **InternalJiuJitsu.com** and on Medium. He is a graduate of NYU's journalism program.

www.ingramcontent.com/pod-product-compliance
Lightning Source LLC
Chambersburg PA
CBHW070144080526
44586CB00015B/1833